God Outside the Box

Richard Harries is the Bishop of Oxford. His many publications include *Questioning Belief* and *Art and the Beauty of God*, which was selected as a book of the year by Anthony Burgess in the *Observer*. He is a Fellow of the Royal Society of Literature.

With thanks to
Jim, Martin, Andrew, Ed and Michael
for their support

God Outside the Box

Why spiritual people object to Christianity

RICHARD HARRIES

Published in Great Britain in 2002 by
Society for Promoting Christian Knowledge
Holy Trinity Church
Marylebone Road
London NW1 4DU

British Library Cataloguing-in-Publication Data
A catalogue record for this book is available from the British Library

ISBN 0-281-05522-X

Designed and typeset by Kenneth Burnley, Wirral, Cheshire
Printed in Great Britain by Antony Rowe Ltd, Chippenham, Wilts

Contents

Acknowledgements

Every effort has been made to trace and acknowledge copyright holders of material reproduced in this book. The publisher apologizes for any omissions and, if notified, will ensure that full acknowledgements are made in a subsequent edition.

The author and publishers would like to acknowledge with thanks permission to use extracts from the following material:

W. H. Auden, 'The Truest Poetry is the Most Feigning' (p. 148) from *Collected Poems*, Faber and Faber, 1976.

Louis de Bernières, from a private letter to the author (p. 3).

T. S. Eliot, 'The Dry Salvages' (pp. 31, 157), 'Little Gidding' (pp. 110–11, 112) and 'East Coker' (p. 157) in 'The Four Quartets' from *The Complete Poems and Plays*, Faber and Faber Ltd, 1969.

Eucharistic Prayer G (pp. 17, 64) from *Common Worship*, Church House Publishing, 2000.

D. H. Lawrence, 'Stand up!' (p. 12) from *The Complete Poems*, Vol. 1, ed. Vivian De Sola Pinto and Warrant Roberts, Heinemann, 1964. Used by permission of Laurence Pollinger Ltd and the Estate of Frieda Lawrence Ravagli.

Janet Morley, 'Eucharistic Prayer for Ordinary Use' (p. 17) from *All Desires Known*, Movement for the Ordination of Women and Women's Theology, 1988.

Edwin Muir, 'One Foot in Eden' (pp. 159, 170) from *Collected Poems*, Faber and Faber, 1960.

Wilfred Owen, extract from 'Maundy Thursday' (p. 96) from *The Collected Poems*, edited by C. Day Lewis (1963) published by Chatto and Windus. Used by permission of the Estate of Wilfred Owen and The Random House Group Limited.

C. H. Sisson, 'A Letter to John Donne' (pp. 118, 123) from *Collected Poems*, Carcanet Press Limited, 1984.

Stevie Smith, 'How do you see?' (p. 20) from *Collected Poems*, Allen Lane, 1975.

Rabindranath Tagore, *Gitanjali* (p. 51) from *Collected Poems and Plays*, Macmillan, 1958. Used by permission of Visva-Bharati University, Kolkata, India.

R. S. Thomas, 'The Empty Church' (p. ix); 'The Minister' (p. 96) from *Song of the Year's Turning*, Rupert Hart-Davis, 1955; 'The Priest' (p. 122) from *Collected*

Poems 1945–1990, Dent, 1993; 'The Absence' and 'Abercuawg' (pp. 156–7) from *Frequencies*, Macmillan, 1978; 'Via Negativa' (pp. 156–7) from *H'm*, Macmillan, 1972; 'Suddenly' (pp. 156–7) from *Later Poems*, Macmillan, 1983.

Charles Williams, 'Apologue on the Parable of the Wedding Garment' (p. 140) from *The Image of the City*, Oxford University Press, 1958. Used by permission of David Higham Associates.

Adam Zagajewski, 'Try to Praise the Mutilated World' (p. 161), tr. Claire Cabanagh, originally published in the *New Yorker*, 24 September 2001.

Some of the chapters in this book were delivered when I was Visiting Professor at Liverpool Hope University College, and I would like to express my thanks both for the invitation and the engaged audience.

Introduction

> They laid this stone trap
> for him, enticing him with candles,
> as though he would come like some huge moth
> out of the darkness to beat there.
> Ah, he had burned himself
> before in the human flame
> and escaped, leaving the reason
> torn.[1]
>
> (R. S. Thomas)

> I have a sense of spirituality. I want Brooklyn christened but I don't
> know into what religion yet.
>
> (David Beckham)

In that verse by R. S. Thomas the Church is thought of as a trap from
which God has escaped. This expresses the experience of many people
today. What goes on in church is meaningless to them and traditional
Christian language has gone dead. At the same time they think of themselves as spiritual people with occasional moments of insight through
nature, art or human love. Or, to change the metaphor, the Church has put
God into a box of a particular size, wrapped it in brown paper and tied the
string. But God is outside the box, and many people have discovered this
in their own spiritual yearnings and gropings.

In December 1999 there was a major poll undertaken by Opinion
Research Business. It revealed that while 65 per cent of the population still
believe in God, only 28 per cent were willing to affirm that this God was
personal. The other 37 per cent thought of a God in vaguer terms such as
spirit or life force. At the same time, while 27 per cent of those surveyed
were willing to describe themselves as religious, another 27 per cent

claimed to be spiritual. What is even more significant is that while 39 per cent said that they were not religious, only 12 per cent were willing to be described as 'not a spiritual person'. Or to put it the other way round, 88 per cent of the population resisted being called 'not a spiritual person'.

This poll reveals a trend that has been evident for some time now: the growing number of people who are feeling their way towards a spiritual understanding of life but who do not feel at ease with a great deal of traditional religion. This interpretation was borne out in the first part of 2000 by another major poll undertaken in connection with the BBC series *Soul of Britain* which revealed, for example, that well over 50 per cent of the population believe in a soul.

Further analysis of that *Soul of Britain* poll is even more revealing. In 1987 48 per cent of those polled reported a religious or spiritual experience. In 2000, 76 per cent of those polled admitted to this, the vast majority of whom would be non-churchgoers. Indeed, the figure is probably an under-estimate because there were two extra questions to which people could respond in 1987. This huge rise in the percentage of people reporting some kind of spiritual experience took pollsters by surprise. David Hay and Kate Hunt, who carried out the research and analysed it at the University of Nottingham, commented, I think correctly, that there had probably been no great change in the number of people who had had some degree of spiritual awareness.

> What is probably changing is people's sense of the degree of social permission for such experience. Somehow or other (perhaps with the influence of post-modernism) there is a growing feeling that it is acceptable to admit to such awareness, though it is still something most people still feel quite deeply embarrassed about.[2]

There are other interesting aspects of this survey: the timidity with which people spoke about their spirituality; the range of feelings actually covered by the word 'spiritual'; the 'quest mode', the fact that people said they were on a journey whose end was not clear; the reluctance to use traditional religious language; and the desire to talk much more vaguely about 'something there' which at a profound level could be seen as related to the Christian apophatic tradition. Among older people, when religious language was used it was drawn from the Christian meta-narrative; but for those under 40 there were self-constructed theologies.

Those who call themselves spiritual or who resist being described as not a spiritual person include people with a wide range of views such as those who are interested in various forms of meditation, who are members of one of the 500 or more new religions, who are interested in astrology or the occult, or who simply have their own strong sense of personal values and beliefs that they regard as a very private affair. However, the person I particularly have in mind is characterized by the following features. First, a strong set of values epitomized in a care for other human beings, a concern about animals and the environment, and a sense of tolerance towards others of different beliefs. Second, an interest in self-development and self-fulfilment and a willingness to draw from a whole range of sources on the simple principle of using what will sustain the self or feed the soul. Third, great difficulty with many aspects of traditional religion, particularly traditional monotheistic religion, Judaism, Christianity and Islam. In this book I am concerned particularly with those difficulties and especially with the strong negative feelings many people have about the Christian faith. The Christian faith is found offensive by some, and the number of articles that appear in our newspapers expressing that view seems to be on the increase. Yet I believe the Christian faith calls into question many aspects of our contemporary searching spirituality. At its centre is a battered, crucified figure, who raises a question mark against so many of the values and presuppositions of modern life, including some of our most cherished spiritual and moral concerns. At the same time, I think that those on a spiritual search, particularly a search for their true, spiritual self, can find their proper satisfaction and fulfilment in the Christian faith. But this can only come the other side of taking any hostility to the Christian faith seriously.

So at the heart of this book are some of the real feelings which lead people to react negatively to the Christian faith, feelings that are not always articulated. I am concerned with the moral, emotional and spiritual reasons why people find themselves unable to believe or even totally alienated from Christian beliefs. Apart from the problem of suffering, which continues to be the great barrier to faith, and which I discuss in the final chapter, I suspect that behind the philosophical doubts or reasons drawn from the spurious clash of science and religion, there are inchoate feelings of dislike or rejection that have to do with other things altogether. Alec Vidler, in his history of the Church in the nineteenth century, wrote that many of the people who turned away from Christianity in that century did so, not because of the rise of science or biblical criticism, but because 'what it called upon them to believe, with such confidence of its superiority, struck them as morally inferior to their own ethical ideals and standards'.[3]

I believe this judgement to be of profound significance and that it is even more relevant today than in the past. For even until 20 years ago it was widely assumed, despite the protests of atheists and agnostics, that to be a Christian and to be a good person were synonymous: Christianity occupied the high moral ground. This is no longer the case. It is much more widely acknowledged that people can have their own ethical standards and values in the light of which they find the Christian faith, as they have encountered it, wanting. There is a *moral* critique of Christian faith that is far more important than any other kind, for it calls into question Christianity's core convictions, not simply on the grounds that they are unbelievable, but that they are immoral.

Closely linked with the specifically moral critique is a reaction of the emotions and spirit, an instinctive reaction that Christianity, as tradition-ally presented, is somehow anti-life, only for wimps, reinforcing infantile dependency, and so on. All this is felt particularly strongly by those who see themselves as spiritual rather than religious.

This book is concerned with a particular kind of objection to Christian faith. For example, it does not deal with purely philosophical problems. These have often been considered, and I certainly have nothing new to add to the arguments. Nor, except for facing the criticism that religion is essen-tially divisive, am I concerned with the institution of the church. There is no doubt that many people find that what goes on in church is exceedingly boring. Others have experienced insensitive forms of evangelism which have put them off Christianity for life. Too often it seems that Christians do not practise what they preach – that Christians are just a load of hypo-crites, as the saying goes. But Christians do not claim to be morally better than other people. There is a story about Evelyn Waugh which brings this out well. During the war he and Randolph Churchill served in Yugoslavia. They quarrelled continually and after one particularly bitter incident Churchill said to Waugh, 'I thought you were meant to be a Christian and a Catholic', to which Waugh replied: 'And think how much worse I would be if I wasn't.' There are many kinds of objection to the Christian faith but I am concerned in this book with one particular kind, what might almost be called people's gut reaction to the Christianity they have encountered which makes them react against it in a way which is at once emotional, moral and spiritual.

I believe that these criticisms need to be taken with the utmost serious-ness. There is truth in all of them. But there is also something to be said on the other side, or I would not have written this book. My great teacher at Cambridge, Professor Donald MacKinnon, once said that 'apologetics is the lowest form of Christian life'. What I think he despised was any attempt at propaganda – Christianity at the level of a party political broad-cast. He himself pursued the truth relentlessly and unflinchingly. That, he believed, was the Christian way, however uncomfortable. That is the example I would seek to follow. There are some uncomfortable truths to be faced in this book; but there are also truths which can put these criti-cisms in another perspective. I am quite happy to follow 'the lowest form of Christian life' in trying to state these truths as well as the criticism of them. One of the reasons for trying to shed a Christian light on the gut feelings which make people react negatively to the Christian faith is that so often today Christianity is the subject of glib dismissal. Time and again the colour supplement intellectuals who dominate so much of our media, while displaying an extraordinary ignorance for the basic facts of religion, an ignorance that they would regard as inexcusable in any other sphere, continue to disparage religious beliefs with clever quips. The result is that there is very little serious thought about the kind of criticism that is considered in this book. But the starting point for those of us who would like other considerations to be taken into account must be the negative feelings which so many people have as a result of their encounter with Christianity. I take these seriously because they are serious. If we in the Church take such criticisms with the seriousness that they deserve, it may be that in the end we will win a serious hearing for what we have to say in response to them.

As the research quoted earlier indicates, there is a growing category of people who see themselves as spiritual but who are alienated from much traditional religion. Some of these people are actually in the Church, hanging on by their fingertips. Although I hope that this book has something to say to total sceptics, the person I have particularly in mind is someone sympathetic to a spiritual view of life, who has a strong set of values and is concerned in a profound way with self-development but who finds many of the beliefs and assumptions associated with the Christian faith a hindrance rather than a help, and indeed sometimes quite objectionable.

The book is divided into five parts. The first is concerned with the case against God, that he comes across as a despot, a male chauvinist, that he punishes people and seems concerned only with his own praise. The second part faces all those really difficult questions that arise if we believe that God acts in the world. These include questions about why did it all begin in the first place anyway, the fact that God seems to have favourites, the problem of suffering generally and in particular the apparent cruelty in nature, as well as more general issues of science and religion. The third part deals with what we so often perceive as the failures of religion, its divisiveness, the way it seems stuck in the past, its apparent irrelevance when life feels good anyway and the serious doubt about whether it does in fact promote moral maturity rather than immaturity. The fourth part focuses more specifically on problems associated with the Christian life, that it seems too concerned with sin and guilt, that it is anti-life, far too narrow, with no place for truth in other religions or the goodness produced by other religions. Then there is the language of the Eucharist, which seems to imply that we eat God, and a worry that it is only for wimps, not for strong successful people. The final part 'Towards a Spirituality for Today' argues that traditional Christianity has always had a powerful sense of the ultimate mystery of God and that it is vital for the preservation of true religion that this sense is retained. Together with this, there is the para-doxical way in which so many of the greatest Christian thinkers and saints have known the presence of God in and through his apparent absence. According to the Christian faith however, God has made himself present to us in one particular way. He has acted to reconstitute human society around Jesus. It is in this community, with others, and not apart from them, that we begin to discover who we are. This leads into the major, specific concern of people today searching for a new spiritual understanding of life, namely the growth into true selfhood. It is argued that what people are looking for is all there within the Bible and Christian tradition, and that the Christian faith is able to help us discover our true self without the imbalances and distortions that have crept into some modern religious movements.

Finally, I consider the biggest question of all: whether all the suffering and agony in the world is compatible with a belief that behind it is a wise and loving power. For some this is a question that has been given a new urgency by what happened on 11 September 2001 and all that has occurred since then.

RICHARD HARRIES, OXFORD

January 2002

PART 1

The Case Against God

CHAPTER 1

The Despot God

I am longing for the day when Bishops resign *en masse* as a protest against the feckless master they have served so long, with so much misplaced trust. Humans, at least, are capable of nobility and altruism, and this makes us morally superior to God, who would appear to be like an Ottoman sultan. He is an absolute despot who is out of control of his empire, surrounded by sycophants, answerable to no one, drunk with apathy, who demands homage and taxes from his people without offering any services in return.

(Louis de Bernières)[1]

Louis de Bernières, the author of the best-selling novel *Captain Corelli's Mandolin*, wrote an introduction to the book of Job in a new edition of a number of books of the Bible by Canongate. In his introduction Bernières offered a severe moral critique of the kind of God revealed in the book. He argued that 'Although Jesus Christ and a deluge of sophistical theology did much to improve God's image for a few centuries, Job is still winning the argument and the book of Job is still insidiously subversive.'

In my review of his Introduction for the *New Statesman* I sympathized with this protest but argued that the book of Job does not stand on its own: it had to be seen in the light of Jesus on the cross and the revelation of God given there. I sent a copy of that review to Louis de Bernières, together with another amplifying piece I had written on the problem of suffering, and he wrote back a powerful letter, part of which is quoted at the head of this chapter. The criticism he makes is a severe one, which needs to be taken very seriously. As I mentioned in the Introduction to this book, for most of European history the Christian Church has occupied the moral high ground. Even when people began to become atheists or agnostics in the eighteenth century, it was assumed that this was an immoral thing to do and that to be a Christian and to be a good person were one and the same thing.

As Alec Vidler pointed out, during the nineteenth century people began to bring a moral critique to bear on the claims of religion but, even so, people have on the whole hesitated to do this, so widespread is the assumption in our culture that goodness and religious belief go together. Nevertheless, there have been some outspoken souls. During the Second World War Evelyn Waugh served in Yugoslavia with Randolph Churchill, the son of the great Sir Winston. Evelyn Waugh and his friends got so fed up with Randolph Churchill's continual talking that they took him on a bet that he could not read the whole Bible through from beginning to end. They hoped in this way to shut him up for a while but they were greatly disappointed. After every few verses Randolph Churchill would explode: 'God, isn't God a shit.' When I quoted that story a few years ago in a devotional article for a church newspaper, the expletive was expurgated: that was quite under-standable. Nevertheless, Randolph Churchill's blunt, foul-mouthed utterance puts into words what some devout people feel but dare not articu-late. A more sensitive reaction comes from Brian Keenan. When a hostage in the Lebanon, Keenan experienced the reality of God in an overwhelming way and began for the first time in his life to read the Bible seriously. Both he and John McCarthy found great solace in reading the Psalms. However, as Keenan wrote, 'The blood and gore of the Old Testament stories horri-fied me.'[2] And they horrify anyone of moral sensitivity.

Aspects of this moral rejection of God will be discussed in later chapters, for example the view that God sentences people to everlasting punishment, that he has designed this world solely for his praise, that Christianity encourages an infantile dependence, and that in choosing Israel and then the Christian Church he is guilty of the worst kind of favouritism. However, these criticisms of particular aspects of the divine work or character come to a sharp focus in Louis de Bernières' picture of him as 'an absolute despot' and it is easy to see how certain passages of the Bible, taken in isolation, can give this picture, one which must of course be rejected on moral grounds. However, we do need to consider this theme in a historical perspective.

First of all, the Jewish view of God developed in a world that took ruthless rulers for granted. It is an obvious point to make, but nevertheless important to remember, that the social order of the ancient Near East in the eighth century BC was very different from our own. The great body of human international rights law, for example, has only developed since the Second World War. Before our time there was very little talk of human rights, though there was a very proper emphasis upon human responsibil-ities. When trying to picture the ruler of heaven and earth, it was perhaps inevitable that the writers of the Hebrew scriptures should sometimes picture that ruler in all-too-human terms; that they should project their own fears and furies upon him. If we wish to be critical of certain passages in the Hebrew scriptures, the proper comparison is not with the developed insights of our own time but with the comparative literature of the ancient Near East. When that comparison is made, I believe that the Jewish understanding of God reflects some remarkably well developed moral and spiritual insights. For example, the legislation in the scriptures about how slaves were to be treated and how the poor were to be cared for, express, in the circumstances that prevailed at the time, a sense of compassion. This sense of compassion was rooted in an understanding of what they believed God required of them.

Then, against the view of God which pictures him as demanding our unquestioning obedience and as willing to kill and destroy if he does not receive it, there are innumerable passages which offer a very different picture. This is the God of *Hesed*, of loving kindness, the God who will go to any lengths to support and save his people and who wants a similar loving kindness in our relationships with one another. This is a God who is loyal, utterly faithful to his people whatever they do, a God who will never abandon them. This is a theme that runs right through the Psalms as well as many other books of the Bible. For example:

> Thy mercy, O Lord, reacheth unto the heavens: and thy faithfulness unto the clouds.
> Thy righteousness standeth like the strong mountains: thy judgements are like the great deep.
> Thou, Lord, shalt save both man and beast; How excellent is thy mercy, O God: and the children of men shall put their trust under the shadow of thy wings.
> They shall be satisfied with the plenteousness of thy house: and thou shalt give them drink of thy pleasures, as out of the river.
> For with thee is the well of life: and in thy light shall we see light.
> O continue forth thy loving-kindness unto them that know thee: and thy righteousness unto them that are true of heart.
>
> (Psalm 36.5–10, BCP)

One of the great laments running through the Hebrew scriptures is that something has gone terribly wrong with the world. Repression, injustice, cruelty and killing are everywhere. This means that the devout person in Israel, who quietly goes about trying to do good, is likely to suffer from the rapacity of those who are out for themselves at the expense of others. It also means that the people of Israel as a whole, sandwiched between the great power struggles of the Assyrians and Egyptians, the Babylonians, Persians, Greeks and later the Romans, have little chance to develop their own God-directed life undisturbed. So the people as a whole cry out for deliverance, as do the individual just people within the community. If this is the great lament, the great hope is that God will indeed act to put right everything that is wrong in this world, that he will deliver the righteous poor person. He will rescue the people of Israel from its oppressive neighbours and establish a reign of justice and peace, in which his glory will irradiate all things as they flourish as intended. If sometimes this picture has been perverted into that of a despot acting with peevish revenge, because of all-too-human projections, we need to see that behind that distortion is a deep conviction, a conviction which is fundamental to human existence. It is that the universe is grounded in a moral order and in the end goodness will be revealed in all its goodness and what is evil will be destroyed. This may be dismissed as a pious illusion, mere wishful thinking; but it is a profoundly moral conviction.

For a Christian, this understanding of God's purpose and ways comes to its focus and climax in Jesus Christ. In Jesus, God himself comes among us and ends up on the cross.

> Have this mind among yourselves, which is yours in Christ Jesus, who, though he was in the form of God, did not count equality with God a thing to be grasped, but emptied himself, taking the form of a servant, being born in the likeness of men. And being found in human form he humbled himself and became obedient unto death, even death on a cross. (Philippians 2.5–8)

The eternal Son of God comes among us to break down the barriers of pride and suspicion. Through his very weakness he disarms our hostility and draws us into a new relationship with himself. On the cross Jesus cried out 'My God, my God, why hast thou forsaken me?' Simone Weil, the remarkable French philosopher and mystic, wrote in relation to those words: 'There we have the real proof that Christianity is something divine.'[3] It is the powerlessness of God, the vulnerability and sense of abandonment of Jesus, in a world dominated by coercion and power, that wins our allegiance.

When we contemplate the creator of this vast and mysterious universe, and the unimaginable powers locked up in each atom, it is easy to feel threatened. When we realize that we can only know God as one who, by definition, makes a total difference to our lives, because God is God, not a piece of material or knowledge that we can stand over and scrutinize, then of course we feel threatened. Austin Farrer once put it in a sermon:

> The universal misuse of human power has the sad effect that power, however lovingly used, is hated. To confer benefits is surely more godlike than to ask them; yet our hearts go out more easily to begging children than they do to generous masters. We have so mishandled the sceptre of God which we have usurped, we have played provi-

dence so tyrannically to one another, that we are made incapable of loving the government of God himself or feeling the caress of an almighty kindness. Are not his making hands always upon us, do we draw a single breath but by his mercy, has not he given us one another and the world to delight us, and kindled our eyes with a divine intelligence? Yet all his dear and infinite kindness is lost behind the mask of power. Overwhelmed by omnipotence, we miss the heart of love. How can I matter to him? we say. It makes no sense; he has the world, and even that he does not need. It is folly even to image him like myself, to credit him with eyes into which I could ever look, a heart that could ever beat for my sorrows or joys, a hand he could hold out to me. For even if the childish picture be allowed, that hand must be cupped to hold the universe, and I am a speck of dust on the star-dust of the world.

Yet Mary holds her finger out, and a divine hand closes on it. The maker of the world is born a begging child; he begs for milk, and does not know that it is milk for which he begs. We will not lift our hands to pull the love of God down to us, but he lifts his hands to pull human compassion down upon his cradle. So the weakness of God proves stronger than men, and the folly of God proves wiser than men. Love is the strongest instrument of omnipotence, for accomplishing those tasks he cares most dearly to perform; and this is how he brings his love to bear on human pride; by weakness not by strength, by need and not by bounty.[4]

It is in the light of this understanding of God that all other pictures must be judged. This is not to draw a great wedge between the Old and New Testaments, as some have done in the past, thinking that the Old Testament gives us an angry God of justice and the New Testament a God of love. On the contrary, as I have already argued, at the heart of the Hebrew scriptures is a God of *Hesed*, of loving kindness, who will act to vindicate those who act with the loving kindness that reflects his own nature and being. The picture of God given us in Jesus, his teaching and life, builds upon and draws into a focus the best insights of the religion into which he was born and by which he was shaped.

It has to be said that the Christian Church has not always done this. Too often it has reverted to a very human picture of God acting like any human ruler. But in recent years the understanding of God given us in Jesus Christ has more and more been allowed to shape the whole of Christian theology. For example, for too long there was an unconscious assumption that God could simply, as it were, create with effortless ease. W. H. Vanstone in *Love's Endeavour, Love's Expense*,[5] argued on the contrary that God pours himself into creation, he expends himself to the uttermost. It is not just on the cross that God is drained. In creation itself, nothing is held back.

In the light of this we can therefore ask about the roots of the critique of God given by Louis de Bernières and others. Is not this moral criticism of God ultimately drawn from the moral insights given in European culture by the spirit and influence of Jesus Christ?

The historian Herbert Butterfield pointed out many years ago now that the rise of science in the West owed a very great deal to the Christian understanding of nature. In contrast to some cultures, where nature is regarded as being in the hands of unpredictable gods who act in an arbitrary manner, Christianity has a doctrine of creation. God gives the created order a real independence, with its own rhythms and regular patterns. It is because of this autonomy and those observed regularities which we call laws of nature that science is able to develop. For science depends upon the ability to make predictions about the future on the basis of the observed regularities of the past. So although the whole scientific enterprise since the eighteenth century has sometimes been regarded as a foe to Christianity, in fact its success was made possible by the understanding of creation and nature provided by Christian philosophy.

In a similar way, the kind of moral critique of religion that we now have in the modern world is made possible because of moral insights given us in the teaching, life and death of Jesus Christ. The Church, in putting forth its picture of God, has not always been faithful to those insights; it has indeed been open to criticism. Nor need we or should we refrain from bringing moral criticism to bear upon certain passages in the scriptures. But if we take the scriptures as a whole and particularly the picture of God given us by and through Jesus Christ, we have a standard in the light of which all other views can be seen.

> At that time Jesus spoke these words: 'I thank thee, Father, Lord of heaven and earth, for hiding these things from the learned and wise, and revealing them to the simple. Yes, Father, such was thy choice. Everything is entrusted to me by my Father; and no one knows the Son but the Father, and no one knows the Father but the Son and those to whom the Son may choose to reveal him.
>
> 'Come to me, all whose work is hard, whose load is heavy; and I will give you relief. Bend your necks to my yoke and learn from me, for I am gentle and humble-hearted; and your souls will find relief. For my yoke is good to bear, my load is light.' (Matthew 11.25–30)

In the light of this understanding of God disclosed in Jesus Christ it is not surprising that the Bible has been an inspiration to so many in resisting tyranny. The New Testament itself is subversive of all regimes built upon privilege; for it proclaims that the world will be turned upside down, with the last becoming first and the first last. This is the theme sung at the birth of Jesus in the Magnificat:

> He hath shewed strength with his arm: he hath scattered the proud in the imagination of their hearts.
> He hath put down the mighty from their seat: and hath exalted the humble and meek.
> He hath filled the hungry with good things: and the rich he hath sent empty away.

This is a theme exemplified in every age: in the early centuries of the Church when bishops stood up to emperors; in the fourteenth century when the priest, John Ball, led the Peasants' Revolt with the words 'When Adam delved and Eve span, who was then the gentleman?' The great Dr Johnson is sometimes caricatured as a Church of England Tory, conservative in all his thoughts and ways. But as Boswell recalls, to his own distaste Johnson 'had always been very zealous against slavery in every form'. 'Upon one occasion, when in company with some very grave men at Oxford, his toast was, "Here's to the next insurrection of the Negroes in the West Indies".'[6]

In our own time we have the example of the liberation theologians who encourage communities of the poor to stand up for themselves and oppose all forms of economic and political oppression. This has brought forth its own martyrs, such as Archbishop Oscar Romero, while in Africa Archbishop Luwum lost his life for opposing the tyranny of Amin.

So if it is true that despotic regimes have sometimes drawn from the Bible a picture of God as a despot to reinforce their own ruthless rule, no less is it true that people have drawn on the picture of God in Jesus Christ and all that points to this in the Hebrew scriptures in order both to oppose tyranny and reinstate a very different picture of God from the one given by despotic regimes. There have always been those who, standing alongside the poor, opposed what William Blake called the 'nobodaddy' – nobody's daddy.

It is understandable and perfectly appropriate, indeed morally essential, that people react against certain pictures of God, even some pictures presented in the scriptures. But God is not like that. He is much more like the Jesus in some of Rembrandt's later paintings. In the early stages of his career Rembrandt painted in a grandiose, baroque manner. After his family died and he got into great financial trouble his whole style of painting changed. He painted Jesus as an almost diminutive figure hidden in the midst of the crowd who seek his healing and help. For many today, having rejected the despot God, the one they are looking for seems silent and hidden, but as John Updike has written, 'A loud and evident God would be a bully and a tyrant . . . instead of, as he is, a bottomless encouragement to our faltering and frightened being.'

CHAPTER 2

The Male Boss

Man corrupt everything . . . he tried to make you think he everywhere. As soon as you think he everywhere, you think he God, but he
ain't. Whenever you trying to pray and man plop himself on the other
end of it, tell him to git lost.
        (Celie in *The Color Purple* by Alice Walker)[1]

The criticism which we have to face in this chapter has two, interrelated
aspects. The first is that Christianity is irreformably hierarchical and
authoritarian in a world which is increasingly egalitarian and consensual.
The second is that it is irredeemably patriarchal. In a world in which the
role of women is being increasingly valued and promoted, Christianity
remains committed to an understanding of God and a view of religion
which is not only authoritarian and hierarchical but chauvinist. In terms of
Alice Walker's Celie, when women are trying to pray they find a male figure
intruding at the other end of the line as it were. He needs to be told to get
lost. In short, Christianity seems committed not only to a supreme boss
figure and bosses all the way down, but a male boss and male bosses all the
way down. This is no longer acceptable.

The criticism of this kind of religion takes a number of different forms.
There is the critique which exposes it as a method of social control. Christianity is committed to hierarchy on this view because it has been used by
and associated itself with the dominant class. Churches have very often
been state churches, in league with royalty and the aristocracy. From this
we get Lenin's description of priests as simply 'gendarmes in cassocks'.
The dominant class uses the Church for social control, not only through
the message it delivers through the pulpit, but through ensuring that the
Church's message of submission and obedience is internalized and becomes
part of people's conscience. In addition to this – mainly – Marxist social
analysis there is a no less powerful moral critique. According to this view

the ideal human community is one that exists on the basis of equality and mutual respect. Everyone is equally valued and the contribution of all is welcomed, none more than another. There is a moving description of this ideal in the early chapters of the Acts of the Apostles:

> They met constantly to hear the apostles teach, and to share the common life, to break bread and to pray . . . All whose faith had drawn them together held everything in common: they would sell their property and possessions and make a general distribution as the need of each required. With one mind they kept up their daily attendance at the temple, and, breaking bread in private houses, shared their meals with unaffected joy, as they praised God and enjoyed the favour of the whole people. (Acts 2.42–47)

Many times in the course of Christian history groups of people have got together, in reaction to a corrupt, power-hungry Church, in order to recreate this ideal of communal Christian living. It emerged again in secular form during the 1960s, when a great number of communes were founded.

Then there is the psychological criticism. This focuses on the fact that a hierarchical, authoritarian system is likely to be internalized, leading to emotional repression. So people need to be liberated internally from Christianity, as well as socially and politically.

To these criticisms is now added the one from the feminists which reinforces the previous negative reactions while emphasizing all the time that it is women who suffer most. In any system of social control they are the ones at the bottom of the pile. In any hierarchical system they are the ones who will have to bear the majority of the burdens and whose contribution will be least publicly valued. They are the ones most likely to internalize this repressive regime, leading to a lack of self-esteem and lack of confidence in pushing for basic human rights. It is not surprising therefore that some feminists, once Christian, no longer see themselves in that way. Daphne Hampson, for example, has written:

> Having wanted to be ordained for 20 years, I left the church in which I could be only a second-class citizen. In time, I found I could no longer read my Bible. Then I ceased to be a Christian, for something dawned on me: that Christianity is a masculinised religion and irreformable. My fear is now, with the ordination of women, the depth of the problem will not be apparent . . . If God is good, then God cannot be held to will an ideology that damages women. Nor can there have been a revelation of God which should, for two millennia, have promoted a hierarchy based on gender. Christianity

may be a myth that has carried human religious consciousness, but it is a myth that is no longer acceptable.[2]

D. H. Lawrence once wrote a poem parodying a famous hymn:

> Stand up, but not for Jesus!
> It's a little late for that.
> Stand up for justice and a jolly life.
> I'll hold your hat.
>
> Stand up, stand up for justice,
> ye swindled little blokes!
> Stand up and do some punching,
> give 'em a few hard pokes.
>
> Stand up for jolly justice,
> you haven't got much to lose:
> a job you don't like and a scanty chance
> for a dreary little booze.
>
> Stand up for something different,
> and have a little fun,
> fighting for something worth fighting for
> before you've done.
>
> Stand up for a new arrangement,
> for a chance of life all round,
> for freedom, and the fun of living
> bust in, and hold the ground![3]

In that poem, he brings out well, in popular form, the political, moral and psychological liberation that is necessary from certain forms of Christianity. But it was of course written before the advent of the feminist movement and the emphasis is upon 'swindled little blokes' rather than subjugated women.

These criticisms are very telling and the large element of truth in them has simply to be recognized, faced and accepted. But fairness demands that we unpick these criticisms and separate them into their different strands. Not all strands are equally unacceptable and there may be some strands which, far from being unacceptable, are in fact essential to any kind of human living together.

For most of human history, not only in Europe, hierarchy was accepted not just as a necessity but as a noble ideal. At the top is God, King of kings and Lord of lords. Below him is the king, sometimes regarded as a sacred or almost sacred figure. Below that are the nobles, squires and common folk. This was all presented in a glorious light with an emphasis upon the religious duty of obedience. But it was also recognized that, whether or not this structure had a religious glamour to it, it was certainly essential for human society. In Shakespeare's play *Troilus and Cressida*, Ulysses sees the whole cosmos, including the planets, held together by hierarchy and disorder only erupting when this is challenged:

> Take but degree away, untune that string,
> And hark what discord follows. Each thing melts
> In mere oppugnancy. The bounded waters
> Should lift their bosoms higher than the shores
> And make a sop of all this solid globe;
> Strength should be lord of imbecility,
> And the rude son should strike his father dead;
> Force should be right; or rather, right and wrong,
> Between whose endless jar justice resides,
> Should lose their names, and so should justice too.
> Then everything includes itself in power,
> Power into will, will into appetite;
> And appetite, an universal wolf,
> So doubly seconded with will and power,
> Must make perforce an universal prey
> And last eat up himself.[4]

This passage suggests that without hierarchy life will be nothing but an anarchic struggle for power. There will be total chaos, in which might will be the only measure and as a result of which human community will be totally destroyed. Sadly, that is indeed the situation in some countries where law and order have totally broken down. Every organization knows that there needs to be some element of structured hierarchy. This is obvious in the armed services but it is no less present in any business. Decisions have to be made, people have to take responsibility for them, those decisions have to be followed through and there needs to be some element of control. In short, there needs to be management and a board of directors, and if people fail to carry out what is required of them, they lose their job. What applies in business is equally applicable to government and civic life. No society can exist without government and all governments must retain enough power in order to avoid anarchy, even if that power is of a relatively benign kind, like the traditional bobby on the beat.

What has changed in the modern world, however, is that we no longer find it acceptable for these hierarchies to be maintained on a hereditary basis. Those who make decisions on behalf of other people, whether it is for a company or a local community, must be in their position because of personal ability. Our society may still be beset by class considerations but in principle we believe in equality of opportunity for all.[5]

The other dramatic change that has taken place in our society is what has been termed the 'decline in deference'. People today prefer an informal style. This can be seen in some of our most successful international companies. Although there is a hierarchy, everyone is on Christian name terms, there are the minimum of perks and privileges for senior executives, and such companies try to give equal respect to everyone who is employed, taking full account of the particular contribution they can make.

It might be possible for very small communities to exist without any hierarchy at all. But the attempts in the 1960s to build communes on this basis resulted in a number of spectacular failures. They experienced the division and fragmentation that characterizes all human attempts to live together. A more telling example is that of the Benedictine community, which has survived and flourished since the sixth century. The Benedictine rule is a judicious mixture of idealism and common sense. There is a hierarchy but the Abbot is elected, preferably chosen unanimously by the whole community. He has power but the rule makes it quite clear that his responsibilities are to be exercised with a very particular kind of gentleness:

> Let him always distrust his own frailty and remember that the bruised reed is not to be broken . . . Let him study rather to be loved than feared. Let him not be turbulent or anxious, overbearing or obstinate . . . Let him so temper all things that the strong may still have something to long after, and the weak may not draw back in alarm.[6]

For Christians the model of leadership is authoritatively given in Jesus. Once James and John asked that they might sit in state in the coming kingdom of God. Afterwards, the other ten were indignant about this request and Jesus taught them:

> 'You know that in the world the recognized rulers lord it over their subjects, and their great men make them feel the weight of authority. That is not the way with you; among you, whoever wants to be great must be your servant, and whoever wants to be first must be the willing slave of all. For even the Son of Man did not come to be served but to serve, and to give up his life as a ransom for many.' (Mark 10.42–45)

The universe only exists because the infinite wisdom and goodness behind it decided that it should. Our existence is not a mistake or tragic accident: it is the wisest and most loving thing that could happen. In recognizing this we are recognizing that a proper degree of authority belongs to that infinite wisdom and goodness. But that authority is exercised in service. The wisdom of God has come among us in Jesus. He is our brother, relating to us as one of us that he might take us into an eternal relationship with his heavenly Father and ours. As the risen Christ told Mary Magdalene, 'Go to my brothers, and tell them that I am now ascending to my Father and your Father, my God and your God' (John 20.17).

So we need to distinguish between hierarchy and the manner in which that hierarchical rule is exercised. Hierarchy is not only essential for the running of any human organization and society; it belongs to the structure of the universe because all things spring forth from that ultimate mystery who is the source and standard of all value. But in Jesus we are given the definitive example of how this authority is to be expressed, in the service of others. The modern emphasis upon equality, the doing away of perks and privileges, the decline in deference and so on, all indicate a major shift, not away from hierarchy as such, but towards a more Christian understanding of it.

If this understanding of hierarchy is not only acceptable but regarded as a positive good, there remains the fact that for all history hierarchy has been associated with male power. Male power, conceived hierarchically, has been used to oppress and subjugate women in so many ways, not least in religion. In recent decades a number of writers have sought to rectify this situation. First of all there is an awareness of the male bias, and the sheer horror of this as exhibited. So it is necessary to look at those stories in the Bible where women have had the most terrible things done to them. From this has come a capacity to read the Bible from a woman's point of view. This means not only reading it with an awareness of the horrendous way in which women were too often treated, it also means a retrieval of those stories where women are presented in a much more positive role. These are stories which over the centuries have been ignored by predominantly male exegetes. In addition to this new way of reading the Bible there has been an attempt to use inclusive language in the reading and liturgy of the Church. Although this has been resisted in some quarters, for many church people it is now natural to use inclusive language and there is an instinctive reaction against some of the old exclusive language. A fundamental shift in consciousness is in the process of taking place.

Much more controversial is the imagery which we use of God and the personal pronouns which are used in connection with the Creator. Here again progress has been made. There are references to Christ as mother in a number of Church Fathers and the Holy Spirit has sometimes been thought of as feminine in Christian tradition. In the Bible itself the feminine dimension of God can also be seen. In the Wisdom literature for example, divine wisdom is conceived of as feminine and is written about in passages of great beauty:

> For she is a breath of the power of God,
> and a pure emanation of the glory of the Almighty;
> therefore nothing defiled gains entrance into her.
> For she is a reflection of eternal light,
> a spotless mirror of the working of God
> and an image of his goodness.
> Though she is but one, she can do all things;
> and while remaining in herself, she renews all things;
> in every generation she passes into holy souls
> and makes them friends of God, and prophets;
> for God loves nothing so much as the man who lives with wisdom.
> For she is more beautiful than the sun,
> and excels every constellation of the stars.
> Compared with the light she is found to be superior,
> for it is succeeded by the night
> but against wisdom evil does not prevail.
> She reaches mightily from one end of the earth to the other,
> and she orders all things well.
>
> I loved her and sought her from my youth,
> and I desired to take her for my bride,
> and I became enamoured of her beauty.
>
> (Wisdom of Solomon 7.25–8.2)

There remains the fact that in the New Testament the one whom Jesus reveals is addressed as Father and he himself is disclosed as the eternal Son. Although God in himself is neither male nor female and in his perfection includes in sublime, perfected form all that we associate with concepts of the masculine and the feminine, the language of revelation about God is, for the most part, irrefutably masculine. This is an aspect of Christian tradition that cannot be side-stepped. Nevertheless, while this will remain true, it is perfectly orthodox to qualify this language with images associated more with the feminine. All images of God have continually to be qualified, to be denied as well as affirmed, and masculine imagery about God is no exception.

It is basic to Christian belief that God has united himself to humanity in and through a particular person. One of the consequences of the incarnation is that Jesus is necessarily a particular person, at a particular place in time, with a particular gender and, for example, a particular skin and hair colour. Fair-haired people don't feel excluded by Christ's dark hair because there is no history of oppression by dark-haired people of those with fair hair. In other words, it is the subsequent history of oppression of women that gives Christ's gender its significance and not something problematic about the particularity of his gender per se. Thus the problem is in how the Church specifically and the culture generally have deployed gender politics. Christ's gender is made problematical by the significance subsequently attached to it. It is also important to note that Christ's attitude towards women, the welcome he gave them and the way he treated them as instanced in so many stories in the gospels, was subversive of the sexist gender politics of his day.

Our understanding of God inevitably draws on images of human power structures, which historically have been male dominated. For example, in the medieval period perceptions of God paralleled feudal overlordship. Since the nineteenth century with its welfare reforms, a more benevolent image of God has emerged. What is happening now is that the changing role of women in our society is changing our perceptions in many ways, and altering both our language and mental image of God. All this can be done in an entirely orthodox way. For example, a paragraph in a eucharistic prayer that has found much support in ecumenical circles and which is now part of Eucharistic Prayer G in the Church of England's new *Common Worship* reads:

How wonderful the work of your hands, O Lord!
As a mother tenderly gathers her children
You embraced a people as your own.[7]

Janet Morley has produced many fine prayers and liturgies which, while remaining entirely orthodox, recognize the proper place of women. For example, a paragraph in her eucharistic prayer for ordinary use reads:

Therefore, with the woman who gave you birth,
The women who befriended you and fed you,
Who argued with you and touched you,
The woman who anointed you for death,
The women who met you, risen from the dead,
And with all your lovers throughout the ages,
We praise you saying:[8]

A few years ago I took a party of young people to the ecumenical Christian community at Taizé in France. One of the brothers took as his Bible exposition for the week the parable of the prodigal son.[9] In this story which concentrates on the role of the father, the prodigal and the elder brother we might ask: where is the mother? In answer to that question one child replied that in the parable 'The father loves like a mother.' The Taizé brother focused on these feminine characteristics in the parable for the whole week, looking in particular at Rembrandt's great painting of the prodigal son kneeling before the father, who embraces him. This is indeed the theme of Henri Nouwen's now widely appreciated book *The Return of the Prodigal Son*. The book consists of a sustained meditation on Rembrandt's painting, drawing out the feminine element and highlighting their meaning.

So although the pain and anger of women when they read the Bible or encounter a male-dominated Christian liturgy is entirely understandable, it is not true that Christianity is irreformable. The process of change has of course only just begun, but what has been achieved in even two decades is encouraging and significant for the future. Furthermore, as women come to play an increasingly important role in the leadership of the Church, this experience will not only qualify traditional perceptions of the divine mystery but will enlarge and enrich them. It is part of the experience of history as well as of the faith of the Church that Christian tradition has a capacity to renew itself, or rather be renewed by the Holy Spirit, in each age. This is already happening in our understanding of hierarchy, which again is being very much influenced by the experience of women's ministry and the gifts they are bringing to bear.

At Shiraz Airport in Iran many young people congregate to talk to arriving passengers and improve their English. One group of 13-year-old girls came up to me and in very good English asked me what I did. I replied that I was a kind of Christian Imam. One girl then continued the conversation by suggesting that God is not a 'he' or a 'she' or an 'it'. I agreed and said that I thought that all that is meant by 'he' and 'she' and 'it' is contained in their fullness within the Godhead. The girl then gave me a delightful little sermonette on the fact that God is love and we should love one another. We were agreed, this 13-year-old Muslim girl and myself, that strictly speaking God is beyond gender or, more positive, all that we mean by gender is contained in him in complete form. But Christianity has come down to us with predominantly masculine images and we need to rediscover in our own tradition images which balance these with the feminine. C. F. Andrews, the great Christian priest, friend of Gandhi, wrote to Rabindranath Tagore and mentioned how mother love had always been the strongest factor in his life. He went on to say:

> It was the mother in you that was drawing me, even when I felt the mother in me going out to you. It is the woman in one, in the very heart of manhood when it is fullest and strongest and best, that is deepest of all, and goes back to God himself.[10]

Andrews also wrote to his close Hindu friend Munshi Ram to say 'I join with you in the early morning quiet, and my heart meets your heart and the heart of the Universal Mother has bound us, Her children, together in love.'[11] One of the fundamental experiences of interfaith dialogue is that making the journey into a greater understanding of another person's faith at the same time leads to a deeper journey into one's own faith where buried treasures are unearthed. So as Bishop Lakshman Wickremesinghe of Sri Lanka said:

> The feminine principle is no doubt portrayed in Christian scripture, and further developed in the writing of the Eastern fathers and medi-aeval mystics, but the impact of Hindu insight and devotion leads to a more far-reaching appreciation of its pervasiveness in the life of God and man.[12]

Within Christianity we are only at the early stages of this discovery.

CHAPTER 3

Eternal Punishment

And the penal sentences of Christ: He that believeth
And is baptized shall be saved, he that believeth not
Shall be damned. Depart from me ye cursed into everlasting fire
Prepared for the devil and his angels. And then
Saddest of all the words in scripture, the words,
They went away into everlasting punishment. Is this good?
(Stevie Smith)[1]

Stevie Smith is a person who exemplifies the theme of this book. For much of her life she was a devout, high-church Anglican. She loved the Church and the attractive side of Christianity. But the older she got, the more her doubts grew; not simply about the truth of particular doctrines, but about whether Christianity was a force for good or ill in the world. In particular she came to think that certain aspects of Christianity were immoral. She explores this tension most poignantly in her poem 'How Do You See?'. She still felt that Christianity had what she termed 'enchantment' but the moral aspect, not least its belief in everlasting punishment, had, she believed, to be rejected. Nor did she avoid the fact that teaching about everlasting fire appears in the New Testament, reported as coming from Jesus, as the quotation above indicates.

There is no doubt that the Church has held the threat of eternal punishment over people's heads for most of Christian history. This is a belief that has resulted in a good number of terrifying pictures of the Last Judgement, traces of which can still be found on the walls of our medieval churches. Nor is this theme confined to the Western Church, though it receives greater emphasis there. It can be seen in early medieval icons in the monastery of St Catherine at Sinai, as well as in Byzantine mosaics in the church in Torcello, in the Venetian lagoon. It is a doctrine that has inspired great literature, above all of course Dante's great work.

During the nineteenth century people began to react against such a terrifying view. But F. D. Maurice was sacked from his professorship at King's College, London for denying the 'everlastingness' of hell. Although the doctrine does not seem to be much taught these days, Catholics of an earlier generation certainly remember having this fear instilled into them.

It is easy for us to sit light to such a belief today, with our doubts about whether there is an afterlife at all and our inclination to create a liberal God in our own liberal image. But the fear that this belief inspired in people of previous generations should not be underestimated. The poet and hymnwriter William Cowper was a lovely, gentle man. He was also a believing Christian, who had gone through a conversion experience of an orthodox Evangelical kind. Yet he could not shake off the belief that, despite this, he was eternally damned. He went through great periods of depression, in which his only solace was playing with rabbits and other gentle creatures. Dr Johnson was of a more robust temperament than Cowper, but there is a remarkable exchange recorded by Boswell, when Johnson went back to visit his old college, Pembroke, at Oxford:

> Dr Johnson surprised him not a little, by acknowledging with a look of horror, that he was much oppressed by the fear of death. The amiable Dr Adams suggested that God was infinitely good. *Johnson,* 'That he is infinitely good as far as the perfection of his nature will allow, I certainly believe; but it is necessary for good upon the whole, that individuals should be punished. As to an individual, therefore, he is not infinitely good; and as I cannot be sure that I have fulfilled the conditions on which salvation is granted, I am afraid I may be one of those who shall be damned.' (looking dismally) *Dr Adams*, 'What do you mean by damned?' *Johnson* (passionately and loudly), 'Sent to Hell, Sir, and punished everlastingly.' . . . Mrs Adams. 'You seem, Sir, to forget the merits of our Redeemer.' *Johnson,* 'Madam, I do not forget the merits of my Redeemer; but my Redeemer has said that he will set some on his right hand and some on his left.' – He was in gloomy agitation, and said, 'I'll have no more on't.'[2]

What is remarkable is that both Cowper and Johnson belong to the eighteenth century, the age of enlightenment, not the medieval period. While it may be true that both of them were depressives and their periods of depression had physical or psychological roots rather than being the direct result of their Christian beliefs, nevertheless their Christian beliefs were there to be latched on to and may have reinforced their sense of isolation, rejection and depression.

The moral objection to this belief can be stated quite simply. We cannot imagine loving parents subjecting their child to unremitting torture. Even if the child had acted in such a way as to arouse the wrath of its parents, parents who inflict torture would be violating every norm of human rights as set out during this century. We cannot regard as good a God who acts immorally; nor can we evade the issue by saying that the belief belongs to the later Church. While it certainly receives greater emphasis in the late medieval period, as Stevie Smith's quotation shows, its origin lies in the New Testament itself. It is a charge that we need to take with great seriousness. What can be said on the other side?

First it is necessary to define what we might mean by hell or everlasting punishment. I cannot believe that the God and Father of Our Lord Jesus Christ deliberately sentences people to unending fire. This is not just because such a picture totally contradicts any understanding of what it means to love, which is itself a crucially important consideration, but it is contrary to the picture of God given to us by Jesus in the New Testament. The picture which Jesus gives us is of a God who goes out of his way to gather in his lost children. However, this does not mean that hell is unreal. If, coming into the presence of perfect goodness and sublime beauty we turn in on ourselves with a mixture of self-pity and resentment, that is hell. It is not a hell that God has created. He is present with his unqualified love and all-embracing generosity. But people in such a state of mind create their own hell in the midst of heaven. If they persist with that state of mind, then it persists.

If we take seriously the fact that as human beings we are free to choose, then this kind of hell is always a logical possibility. God has given us freedom of choice and he respects that freedom of choice everlastingly. So it is always a logical possibility that a person will reject goodness and turn in on themself. It is not of course that God wills such a hell. It is simply that this is logically entailed by a belief in free will. At the same time, it is not necessary to believe that people are bound to remain in that state for ever. There is always a logical possibility that they will be wooed out of it. Furthermore, if God's love is infinite and everlasting, he never gives up on any of us. Does this mean to say that God will eventually draw every single human being out of their own self-made prisons? That all will be saved, to use the traditional language? We cannot say that for certain, because of what has already been stated about the logical consequence of believing in free choice. But we can always hope and pray and trust that as God's love never gives up on anyone, all will in the end respond. The tension in this position has never been more powerfully explored than in the writings of Julian of Norwich in the fourteenth century, in which, despite what she took to be the Church's clear teaching on the matter, she trembles on the brink of universalism, the belief that God's love will eventually win all souls over.[3]

There are some other considerations which also need to be borne in mind. For example, generations previous to ours were much harsher in their attitude to punishment: they took it for granted as an essential feature of existence. Slaves could be treated mercilessly, children were often beaten at school, while the criminal system exacted severe penalties – hanging and transportation for example – for what we would regard as minor crimes. People for the most part lived in a framework of fear, and this included their understanding of the gods or God as well. In the ancient world people thought of the universe as having three tiers. God was in his heaven above, we were on this earth, and underneath was the abode of the departed, the place of maximum separation from God in his abode above. Because they were familiar with volcanoes and geysers the underworld was seen as a place of torturous heat. Thank God that all this has changed. We have a much more humane attitude to the way children are brought up and educated and, for the most part, the way convicted criminals should be treated. We no longer think of the universe as having three tiers, or the abode of the departed as a place of molten lava. Separation from God, a separation not willed by God himself but perhaps brought about by our own recalcitrance, has to be imagined very differently. Some of this change has been brought about by humanists of a utilitarian cast of mind, particularly during the nineteenth century. But Christians have often been active in these progressive movements to bring about a more humane regime. When Christians did this and when they do it now, they often see what they are doing as a working out of the true meaning and spirit of the gospels.

Another factor to be remembered is that the concept of punishment, in some sense, cannot be totally discarded without also jettisoning any proper role for human responsibility. Actions have consequences and to be a responsible human being means trying to take into account the consequences of our actions and to be responsible for them. Some of our actions have effects which hurt other people. According to a strict moral calculus harmful actions should hurt the person who perpetrates them, not other people. So punishment is, as it were, trying to bring home to someone the harmful effect of something that they have done. It is not meant to be punitive; that is, punishing them for punishment's sake: it is trying to get them to see the effect that they have on others and to take responsibility for what they do. This also can be done in a humane way, as in the very promising concepts of restorative justice now being tried out. This method involves bringing perpetrators of crimes face to face with their victims and making them face up to what they have done.

It would not be immoral to think of the afterlife as a place where restorative justice has a part. Indeed, if the universe is to be regarded as moral, it must be regarded in some such a way. If in the end justice is to prevail and the right is to be vindicated, which is the great theme and hope running right through the Hebrew scriptures, then we will all have to face up to who we are and what we have done before other people and before God. We do now, in some respects, live in a more humane world. Capital punishment has been abolished in the United Kingdom (except for treason) and in some other countries. Corporal punishment is also on its way out. But those who bring up children know that, whether in the home or at school, it is for the good of the child that he or she recognizes certain boundaries, and that if these boundaries are overstepped there are consequences.

The prospect of facing up to who we are and what we have done could be a painful one, which is perhaps why we don't like to think of it very much. It might therefore be useful to approach this subject another way, through the concept of fear. Fear is a fundamental feature of human existence. It is not itself bad; rather, it is a protective device that has evolved in nature. It is because we are fearful of the consequences that we do not put our hand into a fire or run across the road in front of an oncoming vehicle. We are quite properly fearful of the pain that such actions would bring about, and that fear helps us to be prudent. Other ages and other cultures have often been dominated by fear: fear of masters, fear of enemies, fear of disease (especially plagues), fear of death, fear of evil spirits and fear of the gods. As T. S. Eliot put it in a memorable phrase, one taken up by Evelyn Waugh as a title of one of his novels, 'Fear in a handful of dust'.

What is interesting about the teaching of Jesus is that he takes this fear, which people felt, seriously. He does not try to gloss over it or pretend that it was not there. He simply asks, in effect, if we are fearful, what is it that we should truly fear. Then, in a brilliant juxtaposition, Luke adds one of Jesus's most memorable sayings about the way God values each one of us:

> To you who are my friends I say: Do not fear those who kill the body and after that have nothing more they can do. I will warn you whom to fear: fear him who, after he has killed, has authority to cast into hell. Believe me, he is the one to fear.
>
> Are not sparrows five for twopence? And yet not one of them is overlooked by God. More than that, even the hairs of your head have all been counted. Have no fear; you are worth more than any number of sparrows. (Luke 12.4–7)

If we are full of fear, then we need to consider what is the most fearful thing that could happen. The most fearful thing that could happen would be to be cut off for ever from the living God. But if we turn our heart and mind to that living God, we find that we are of infinite value. We need have no fear.

The concept of hell was part of the cultural and mental world in which Jesus grew up and by which he was shaped. This was not the fully developed medieval view but it was nevertheless an abode of the departed where people were cut off from God – and this was painful. Jesus uses such a picture, for example, in his teaching on the rich man and the poor man (Luke 16.19–31). In that parable Jesus brings home to people, through a vivid picture, the crucial importance of actually seeing the suffering of the poor person and responding to it. The poor man was at the rich man's gate day by day. But he simply didn't see him, did not imaginatively take on board that this was a fellow human being, just like himself, but one who was suffering. Such moral and spiritual blindness has severe consequences. There is an urgency about the message of Jesus. He wished to bring home to people the reality of the rule of God and the crucial importance of living under that rule in God's kingdom. That rule is *now*, present in his miracles and teaching, and above all in his person. This sense of urgency is carried over into the whole New Testament. People had to make a decision for it or against it. The first Christians believed that the final crisis of human life was here. God had acted in Jesus to vindicate the devout poor, and his work would shortly be consummated when the humility of God in Jesus would be seen in all its glory – and that glory would show everything up in its true light. It is because of this sense of things coming to a head that we get the kind of statement that Stevie Smith quoted in her poem. In the verse at the head of this chapter she refers to Mark 16.16 and Matthew 25.41. These are indeed hard sayings. But the latter appears in a parable of Jesus which otherwise receives almost universal acclaim today. It is the parable of the sheep and the goats in which the ultimate criterion of judge-ment is whether we have done good or harm to others. Matthew 25.41 continues:

> 'For when I was hungry you gave me nothing to eat, when thirsty nothing to drink; when I was a stranger you gave me no home, when naked you did not clothe me; when I was ill and in prison you did not come to my help.' And they too will reply, "Lord, when was it that we saw you hungry or thirsty or a stranger or naked or ill or in prison, and did nothing for you?" and he will answer, "I tell you this: anything you did not do for one of these, however humble, you did not do for me."'

It is because God loves us that we are here at all. We are here to grow in love, towards God and other people. As we grow in love we grow in a life which nothing can destroy, not even death, and which exists for ever within the everlasting mercy of God. Because things have gone badly wrong on this earth, God himself has come among us in the person of his Son Jesus Christ to save us from what we are doing to one another and ourselves. Time and again the stories Jesus told show the lengths to which

God goes in order to gather us to himself. If parables like those in Matthew 25 bring out the seriousness and the consequences of our choices, this has to be seen against the background of the rest of the New Testament whose emphasis is on the overwhelming love of God going to any lengths in order to bring us to our senses. The cross is of course the measure of that love. This is why in the epistles of the New Testament, written in the light of the total Christian experience, including the resurrection of Christ and the presence with us of the Holy Spirit, although a sense of the seriousness of the choices we make is never lost, the emphasis is on a new-found freedom from fear. For example, St Paul wrote:

> For all who are moved by the Spirit of God are sons of God. The Spirit you have received is not a spirit of slavery leading you back into a life of fear, but a Spirit that makes us sons, enabling us to cry 'Abba! Father!' (Romans 8.15)

Elsewhere, another author writes:

> God is love; he who dwells in love is dwelling in God, and God in him. This is for us the perfection of love, to have confidence on the day of judgement, and this we can have, because even in this world we are as he is. There is no room for fear in love; perfect love banishes fear. For fear brings with it the pains of judgement, and anyone who is afraid has not attained to love in its perfection. We love because he loved us first. (1 John 4.16–19)

The epistle continues by emphasizing that we cannot love God whom we haven't seen unless we also love other people whom we do see. That teaching must always challenge and motivate us. All complacency and self-satisfaction must be banished. At the same time we are to come before God without fear, in trust and love.

There are hard sayings in the New Testament which it is dishonest and sentimental to ignore. They bring home to us the crucial importance of the decisions we make in this life, through which we shape the souls of other people and ourselves. Through our decisions we make ourselves into the people who one day will come into the searing gentleness of divine light when all will be seen for what it is. Jesus was under no illusions about how difficult it is for us to reorder our priorities in order to live under that just and gentle rule of God now. When a man of the ruling class asked Jesus what he needed to do to win eternal life but was not able to do what was asked of him, Jesus said: 'How hard it is for the wealthy to enter the kingdom of God! It is easier for a camel to go through the eye of a needle than for a rich man to enter the kingdom of God.' Those who heard this reply were astonished and appalled. You can almost hear them blurting out 'Then who can be saved?' Jesus replied: 'What is impossible for men is possible for God' (Luke 18.18–27). Again we are left with a tension, a proper tension between the seriousness of the moral life and trust in an all-loving God. If we take seriously the moral claims which life makes upon us then any trace of self-satisfaction and self-righteousness must quickly be eliminated. If we take seriously how much we mean to God then all self-condemnation and fear will be dissolved. St Augustine caught the tension well when writing about the two people crucified either side of Christ: 'Do not despair; one of the thieves was saved. Do not presume; one of the thieves was damned.' Yet that cannot be the final word. The good shepherd continues to search for every lost sheep and 'With God all things are possible'. In his remarkable *Pincher Martin* William Golding describes a man growing in the self-knowledge that he was simply a pair of grasping claws. Then he feels lightning creeping in on him. Some of the lines pointed to the centre, waiting for the moment when they could pierce it. 'Others lay against the claws, playing over them, prying for a weakness, wearing them away in a compassion that was timeless and without mercy.'[4] Golding gets the paradox right when he points out the fact that what is timeless and without mercy is also a compassion.

CHAPTER 4

The Oddness of Praise

I've come across many strange conceptions of deity in my time but
never one before who enjoys being serenaded all day.

(Dean Inge)[1]

Inge was Dean of St Paul's in the 1930s, a well-known figure from his controversial statements in his newspaper columns. As Dean he sat through
many long, musical services. It is alleged that he read detective stories
during this time. At any rate, it is clear from the quotation above that he
found this activity strange and the God implied by it very odd. The same
point was made more recently by Auberon Waugh. After rejecting the
objection to the existence of God that he allows misery and suffering on
earth, he continued:

> A much more serious objection – one that I have seldom, if ever, heard
> discussed – concerns God's purpose in creating humanity and the
> world . . . We are given to understand that our purpose on earth is to
> prepare ourselves in such a way that we can worship, praise and
> adore God for ever . . . No doubt this is true and explains the exis-
> tence of organised religion, but I do not think it provides a very
> satisfactory explanation for the reasons behind creation. It is quite an
> agreeable thing to be praised from time to time. When people say
> 'Well done, Waugh, we thought you produced some decent stuff on
> the servant shortage last week' I am gratified and delighted. But if
> everybody I met – everyone in the world – spent the whole time
> praising me, I would be bored to death and unhappy as a result . . .
> Yet we are asked to believe that God created the world and entire
> universe . . . so that human beings after their terrestrial death could
> spend all eternity praising and worshipping him. What sort of char-
> acter would that reveal?[2]

The criticism could be even more damaging than this. We could say straight out that anyone who wanted to be worshipped by everyone all the time must be an ego-maniac, or at least have such a terrible inferiority complex that they needed this to compensate. This means that any idea that the universe has been brought into existence in order that its creator might be worshipped by its inhabitants now and for all eternity, must be decisively rejected on moral grounds. We would despise any human being who acted in that way, and our feelings cannot be stifled just because this picture is projected onto the deity. So we must say at the outset that God did not create the universe in order to gather millions of worshipping admirers. However, that is not the end of the matter. Perhaps the capacity to appreciate, to admire and in the end to acknowledge the worth of things – their worth-ship – is essential to what it is to be a human being.

There is a great deal of destructive criticism in the modern world, and a culture of distrust and cynicism. No doubt much of this is justified by bitter experience. But if we lose the capacity to appreciate what is of value, something within us dies. There are things of great value in life: the beauty of nature and the miracle of every created thing; sublime works of art; wonderful qualities of friendship and care, and heroic qualities of courage and unselfishness. Without the capacity to recognize and acknowledge these for what they are, life would be bleak and bitter indeed.

If this is admitted, there arises the question about what might be particularly or even supremely worth valuing. As Austin Farrer put it:

> What is the supreme motive of a truth-seeking mind? Is it to explode shams, or to acknowledge realities? . . . After all the detection of shams, the clarification of argument, and the sifting of evidence – after all criticism, all analysis – a man must make up his mind what there is most worthy of love, and most binding on conduct, in the world of real existence. It is this decision, or this discovery, that is the supreme exercise of a truth-seeking intelligence.[3]

This puts the matter in terms of the mind, as was appropriate for a person working in a university environment. But as Cardinal Newman once put it, 'the whole man moves'. We are not just mind: we are emotions and spirit as well. So what happens when we recognize something of value is that we not only give intellectual assent to this value, but our spirit and emotions move out beyond themselves. There can be, in the proper sense of the word, ecstasy, whose Greek roots mean standing out from ourselves. We go out of ourselves, away from our normal introverted self-preoccupied ego, simply to behold what is there with a gaze of appreciation. This gaze will have a spiritual and emotional dimension as well as an intellectual one. There are countless examples of this in everyday experience.

Someone acts kindly towards us; we not only say 'Thank you', we might say 'You *are* good'. There has been a switch away from the benefits of the act to the quality of the person who did it. Or we might be looking at a landscape and after picking out the particular details we like – the light on distant fields, the shape of the clouds or whatever – we simply exclaim aloud 'it's sheerly beautiful'. It is this experience, in supreme degree, to which the practice of religion points. St John of the Cross once asked a visitor what her prayer consisted of and she replied, 'In considering the beauty of God and rejoicing that he has such beauty.' Another example of the same spirit is revealed in the reply of St Francis of Assisi to his friend Leo. Leo was feeling 'down in the dumps' and eventually plucked up courage to ask Francis for advice. Francis simply wrote on a piece of parchment (which is still in existence) all the things he knew about God.

> Thou art the Lord God, triune and one; all good.
> Thou art good, all good, highest good, Lord God living and true.[4]

There does still, however, remain a major problem. Although it might be possible in theory to acknowledge the truth of what has been said so far, it seems that many people in our society have simply lost the capacity to feel like this any more. Auberon Waugh points to the problem when he writes, perhaps as a result of burgeoning democratic ideas, 'People no longer wish to spend all their time praising and worshipping Somebody Else.' There have been fundamental social changes in our culture which result in it being difficult, if not impossible, for many people to get caught up in the praise of something greater than themselves. Yet somewhere, the capacity is there, and it can take dangerous forms, as it did in the Nuremberg rallies in the 1930s in Nazi Germany, as it does sometimes in the chanting of football crowds or the adulation given to pop stars, when thousands of people can be taken up into an orgy of screaming or shrieking. In his book on the history of atheism in the nineteenth century, *God's Funeral*, A. N. Wilson wrote:

> Dethroning God, that generation found it impossible to leave the sanctuary empty. They put man in his place, which had the paradoxical effect, not of elevating human nature but of demeaning it to depths of cruelty, depravity and stupidity unparalleled in human history.[5]

Perhaps this capacity goes deeper than the cultural conditioning given by one particular age. The late Dean of Johannesburg, Gonville ffrench-Beytagh, who was arrested for his opposition to apartheid, was quite clear that as human beings the ultimate choice we have to make is between adoration or suicide. In Peter Shaffer's remarkable play *Equus*, a sick boy, who has blinded horses, is sent to see the doctor, Dysart. Dysart recognizes that in the boy there is a passion, which is indeed totally distorted, but one nevertheless that shows up his own life. Referring to himself he says: 'The finicky, critical husband looking through his art books on mythical Greece, what worship has *he* ever known? Real worship! Without worship you shrink, it's as brutal as that . . .'[6]

One criticism connected with the imagery of praise that is sometimes made, is that if eternity consists of nothing but praise, most of us would be bored stiff. It is not only God who would be bored, as Auberon Waugh suggested, but we ourselves would find it endlessly tedious. This highlights the fact that all the language of religion is metaphor, and metaphors need continually to be qualified. Each metaphor can usually only do one, quite specific job. The metaphor of heaven as endless praise, points to the fact that when we truly admire something, we are taken out of ourselves. We focus on the object and its qualities. Since we are human, the ego can creep in even here. There can be a bit of us which at the same time is admiring the picture of ourselves as admiring, or which is thinking what a clever or cultivated person I am to appreciate this particular work of art. But in true appreciation there is an experience of genuine self-transcendence. The ego is left behind and we simply behold and appreciate. As T. S. Eliot put it, 'You are the music while the music lasts.'[7] In such experiences time has no meaning. So it is not a question of the activity of praise going on for ever and ever, though that is a perfectly possible way of putting it, but of being taken out of ourselves by the beauteous love and loving beauty of the divine, in a moment which is at once timeless and eternal. This is in fact the theme which runs through 'The Four Quartets', T. S. Eliot's great poem, from which the last quotation was taken.

I take seriously the fact that in our culture it is very difficult to get into a frame of mind in which praise of the divine seems either appropriate or natural: for very many people it is strange and alien. But the capacity to appreciate, admire and worship is an essential feature of what it is to be a human being. The current culture of universal mistrust and cynicism is killing off something within us. God does not need our praise, nor did he create us in order that he might be flattered. But we, being human, can recognize what is of value and worth outside ourselves. If, at the heart of the universe, there is that which is the source and standard of all value, then the natural flowering of our capacity to appreciate comes in response to that. We don't praise God in order to gain favour with him or to ingratiate ourselves with the divine. Praise is an expression of thanksgiving, an overflowing of thanks for the love shown to us. Thanksgiving merges into and goes out to praise in reflecting on the source of love, God himself.

The American intellectual Susan Sontag wrote: 'I have always been a great faller-in-love. A great adorer. Bigger than any talent I have, bigger than whatever courage I have, is this desire I have to admire.'[8] I believe that this capacity to appreciate and admire is somewhere within all of us, however deep down. Unfortunately the current climate of systematic suspicion, cynicism and instinctive mistrust makes admissions like that of Susan Sontag all too rare. Yet that capacity is crucial to what it is to be a human being. It may be that many people who think of themselves as spiritual find particular difficulty in the idea of praising God. They are interested in the Eastern religions, with their diffused spirituality, and the idea of a spiritual self which we are here to develop. But, from a Christian point of view, that self develops only insofar as it is able to recognize and respond to glimpses of truth, goodness and beauty outside itself. Those glimpses are glints of a glory that draws us out of prisons of our ego into a sheer radiance.

PART 2

Difficulties In Belief

CHAPTER 5

Why Did It All Begin?

Once granted the first step, I can see that everything else follows –
tower of Babel, Babylonian captivity, Incarnation, Church, bishops,
incense, everything – but what I couldn't see and what I can't see now,
is *why* did it all begin?[1]

(Evelyn Waugh)

Those are words spoken by Mr Prendergast in Evelyn Waugh's novel
Decline and Fall. He is a schoolmaster in the extraordinary establishment
in which the novel is set. He had once been a clergyman but then he had
doubts. It wasn't, he said, the ordinary sort of doubt about Cain's wife or
the Old Testament miracles or the consecration of Archbishop Parker: he
had been taught how to explain all those while he was at college. It was
something deeper than all that. 'I couldn't understand why God had made
the world at all.'

One view popular in the ancient world is that God couldn't, as
it were, help creating. Creations went out from him as a series of emana-
tions or waves from his being. Strictly speaking, of course, these would not
be creations because creation implies an independent, autonomous world,
an existence with a life of its own. If the world is conceived as an emana-
tion of God, then there is no separate existence, all is of God. But Judaism,
Christianity and Islam are united in believing that, in a profound and
important sense, creation is separate from God and has a life of its own.
Furthermore, there is no pre-existent matter on which God works. He
creates *ex nihilo*, out of nothing. And that creation is a deliberate act.

Some modern thinkers have suggested that the universe is a kind of
'play' for God, and this chimes in with certain Hindu views. It is not meant
by this that the universe is a plaything, part of a sport in which God can
do what he likes; rather, the image of play indicates sheer spontaneity, exuberance, enjoying something for its own sake. While there is some truth in

this analogy, by itself it is not adequate. For when we are playing, let us say football or tennis, the balls have no feelings which can get hurt, no thoughts which can experience anguish. We can and do get hurt, terribly hurt. It would seem totally irresponsible for anyone, even God, to create a universe simply out of a sense of play without taking into account the feelings of the sensate creatures he is bringing into existence. Some indeed have suggested the sinister thought that behind the universe there is such a being or there are such beings. As Shakespeare put it in *King Lear*:

> As flies to wanton boys are we to th' gods –
> They kill us for their sport.[2]

Such thoughts are not the preserve of the bitter and cynical. When C. S. Lewis's wife died after their happy but very short marriage he wrote a notebook which was first published anonymously. In this he wrote:

> No, my real fear is not of materialism. If it were true, we – or what we mistake for 'we' – could get out, get out from under the harrow. An overdose of sleeping pills would do it. I am more afraid that we are really rats in a trap or, worse still, rats in a laboratory. Someone said, I believe, 'God always geometrizes'. Supposing the truth were 'God always vivisects'.[3]

This brings out the fact that believers can and sometimes do experience the difficulty of believing more sharply than non-believers. Against the experience that C. S. Lewis recorded Christians set Christ who, to continue the analogy, entered the trap on our behalf. It is above all because of him, in whom God experiences the anguish of the world, that Christians continue to believe that there is a wise and loving power behind the universe rather than a malevolent one. A Jewish rabbi and a Christian priest were once talking about their respective beliefs. The Jewish rabbi said that he could believe in God but couldn't believe the claims Christianity made about Jesus Christ. The priest replied that if it was not for Jesus Christ he would not be able to believe in God.

So, according to Christian faith, the creator of this strange and mysterious universe of ours is good. He creates it out of the goodness of his heart and he has unceasing goodwill to all his creatures. But there still presses the question, why create in the first place? I once switched on the radio and heard an American preacher posing this very question, 'Why did God create the universe?' He then went on, 'God created the world because God was lonely.' This is the direct opposite of orthodox Christianity. Orthodox Christianity states that God is complete in himself. The life of the Godhead is perfect, reciprocal love. In the mutual giving and receiving of the Blessed

Trinity, Father, Son and Holy Spirit, there is complete and perfect felicity. God does not create the world out of his own need. There is no divine well of loneliness waiting to be filled up. This is a theological truth with important emotional ramifications. For we all know in human life how someone who is very emotionally needy can love someone else in a way which can become oppressively demanding. God creates the universe out of the fullness of himself, an overflowing of love, through the Holy Spirit. And this points to an answer to our question as to why God creates. It is the nature of love to create.

The question as to why God created the universe in the first place does not stand alone: a similar question arises in relation to parents and children. Why do parents have children? In the past and still today in Third World countries, there is an obvious practical answer to this question. Parents needed to have a lot of children in order that some of them might survive to look after them in old age. Now in the West, we no longer need to rely on this kind of insurance for our old age. Nor is there the social pressure to have children that there once was. Many couples choose quite deliberately not to have children. So why do the majority make the opposite decision? Again, the answer seems to be that it is the nature of love to create. This is not just true physically, so that the sexual intimacy which is the expression of love brings forth offspring; it is true emotionally and spiritually. Out of love something creative cries to be born. With some couples, that something creative is not always children, for they may not be able to have children. But their love can still be creative in other ways, through service in a Third World country or a commitment to the arts. But whether through children or through some other expression, it is the nature of love to create, to bring into being something other than itself. If a couple become totally absorbed in one another, living only for themselves, there is a love here but it has become distorted, frustrated of its proper expression.

It is the nature of love to create, and the love which creates, creates for the sake of that which is created. To use the human analogy, parents at their best do not create children for themselves; the children are precious in their own right – they are of value in themselves. So it is in the relationship between God and the universe. God creates because he is love and because he is love, he brings things into being for their own sake. He gives them a life of their own, which is what we mean by creation, a life which is worthwhile in itself.

This applies first of all to the natural world. Earlier centuries very often had a sense of the value of creation for its own sake. It was not just seen as a backdrop to the salvation of humanity. Nevertheless it is that latter view which has too often dominated Christian thinking, as though the myriad and miraculous world of plants and animals existed only for us.

But before they exist for us they exist in their own right as their quiet or exuberant, beautiful selves. The modern environmental movement is bringing out this truth in a remarkable way. For why should we move heaven and earth to save a particular species in, say, the Brazilian forest? When we have thousands of different types of butterfly, why should we want to ensure that one particular kind survives? The answer lying behind the huge efforts we are now putting in to conserve the environment is that nature is valuable in itself and this is a silent witness to the religious truth that creation is good.

Sometimes in the evening in summer I see swifts soaring and darting about; hurtling across the sky and then turning with almost unbelievable rapidity before beating their wings and shooting off in another direction. Sometimes they seem to chase one another in pairs, sometimes half a dozen or more flash across the sky. At night they disappear from view and, so it is said, sleep on the wing thousands of feet up. Here is another world, a world apart from me, a world I can only observe and note but cannot get within. What do they think, these swifts, as autumn comes and they move southwards? What do they feel if they find themselves on the ground with their weak legs, a prey to predators? We don't know. Here is a world which is closed to us. But it is a world that is of value in itself, with its own vitality and beauty, its sheer exuberance in being itself.

The world of birds and animals, plants and minerals, was created for its own sake: it is valuable in itself. If this is true of the world of nature, how much more is it true when we come to consider human beings. With us, however, there is one crucial difference: we have the capacity to grow as moral and spiritual beings. Swifts are born, reared, they grow, they fly, they breed and they die. But human life is more than a process of physical growth followed by physical decay ending in death. We have the possibility of spiritual development during our period of both physical growth and, perhaps even more, during our period of physical decline. This spiritual development consists in a growing capacity to transcend the narrow ego and focus on others and their good. In this way we come to reflect the character of God himself. More than this, through this process the very life of God comes to dwell within us and live through us. In Christian thought this has been called the process of divinization or theosis. As the early Church Fathers used to say, God became man in order that we human beings might become divine. Of course we do not become divine in the sense of becoming God. We remain creatures. But it is part of the miracle of God's boundless generosity that he not only creates us but he wants to fill us with his own life, his divine life of love, which opens up to all eternity. This growth into God occurs not just through a greater capacity to live for other human beings, it comes through an ever closer association with God himself. It is said that over the course of a long marriage husbands and wives come to resemble one another. It is sometimes said too that dogs and their owners can bear an uncanny likeness to one another. We are inevitably influenced and shaped by that with which we spend our time. As has been written, 'Here and now, dear friends, we are God's children; what we shall be has not yet been disclosed, but we know that when it is disclosed we shall be like him, because we shall see him as he is' (1 John 3.2).

It is above all the poets who have celebrated the delight of creation in itself and for itself. They have not always been as illuminating in relating this to human beings, whose lives so often seem crabbed and disappointing. An exception was Gerard Manley Hopkins. Few have taken such joy in the richness and variety of creation in all its unusual aspects as Hopkins. He delighted in it for its own sake. At the same time he was able to see that human beings have been created on the same principle, yet with the amazing possibility of becoming more truly themselves, the more they allow themselves to be permeated and filled with the divine life.

> As kingfishers catch fire, dragonflies draw flame;
> As tumbled over rim in roundy wells
> Stones ring; like each tucked string tells, each hung bell's
> Bow swung finds tongue to fling out broad its name;
> Each mortal thing does one thing and the same:
> Deals out that being indoors each one dwells;
> Selves – goes itself; *myself* it speaks and spells,
> Crying *What I do is me: for that I came.*
>
> I say more: the just man justices;
> Keeps grace: that keeps all his goings graces;
> Acts in God's eye what in God's eye he is –
> Christ – for Christ plays in ten thousand places,
> Lovely in limbs, and lovely in eyes not his
> To the Father through the features of men's faces.[4]

This poem, written in the nineteenth century, has an extraordinary modern feel about it. It celebrates the fact that everything in nature, as we say, 'does its own thing'. We human beings are also called to be truly and fully ourselves. The difference between ourselves and the rest of the natural world, however, is that the more Christ fills us, the more richly will we be our true self.

This chapter began with a quotation from Mr Prendergast in Evelyn Waugh's novel. Mr Prendergast, once a clergyman, lost his faith because he simply couldn't see the point of creation. If there was a God, why had it all begun?

I have suggested that the point of creation is itself. It exists for its own sake. It is the nature of love to create, and God is the source and standard of all love. When it comes to human beings we are infinitely precious for our own sake. That is why God, out of his love, has created us. In contrast to the animal world, which glorifies God simply by being itself for its short earthly existence, we have been called to grow and develop, to draw closer to the goal of our longing and to be filled with his life through the Holy Spirit who dwells within us.

CHAPTER 6

Does God Have Favourites?

How odd
Of God
To choose
The Jews.

If a schoolteacher has favourites in class we regard this as immoral. There is a deep-seated sense of fairness in all of us, not least children, that we should be treated equally, particularly by schoolteachers. It therefore seems not only odd, but immoral, that the Creator of the universe should select one group of people for favourable treatment, first the Jews and then Christians. The Jews have always regarded themselves as chosen people. But Christians have had this sense about themselves as well. Indeed in some forms this idea takes on monstrous proportions, as when it is held (as it has sometimes been in the past) that a small minority of the human race are elected before all worlds, predestined to eternal salvation while the vast mass of humanity are nothing but a *Massa damnata*, predestined from all eternity for everlasting fire. But even without such extremes, the whole idea of election arouses suspicion. Yet choosing people can be a proper, morally responsible action.

If a head teacher chooses someone to show visitors around the school, there will be a particular point in this, that may have nothing to do with favouritism. Similarly, if a head teacher chooses a particular pupil to organize a visit to an old people's home or to captain the school team, we recognize that this is entirely appropriate. In such examples people are not being chosen for privilege or for any selfish, personal reasons; they are being chosen to do a particular job in order that the community as a whole might benefit.

It is in this light that we should see the election of the people of Israel. Indeed, this is how they saw themselves in their best moments:

Thus speaks the Lord who is God,
    he who created the skies and stretched them out,
    who fashioned the earth and all that grows in it,
who gave breath to its people,
    the breath of life to all who walk upon it:
I, the Lord, have called you with righteous purpose
    and taken you by the hand;
    I have formed you, and appointed you
    to be a light to all peoples,
    a beacon for the nations,
    to open eyes that are blind,
    to bring captives out of prison,
    out of the dungeons where they lie in darkness.
                           (Isaiah 42.5–7)

The people of Israel saw their election as having a particular purpose, to make the knowledge of God known to all the world, to be a light to enlighten every mind. The Israelites were continually warned not to think that their election by God was due to any merit or quality on their part.

It was not because you were more numerous than any other nation that the Lord cared for you and chose you, for you were the smallest of all nations; it was because the Lord loved you and stood by his oath to your forefathers. (Deuteronomy 7.7)
    When the Lord your God drives them out before you, do not say to yourselves, 'It is because of my own merit that the Lord has bought me in to occupy this land.' It is not because of your merit or your integrity that you are entering their land to occupy it. (Deuteronomy 9.4–5)

In the Hebrew scriptures the people of Israel are chosen not for privilege but for responsibility; not because of their moral qualities but simply because God has chosen them for a particular task – to reveal the knowledge of himself and his purpose to the whole of humanity.

The question arises, however, as to why God does not reveal himself equally to all people. If he wants to be known by all he should disclose himself to all, in every country and every culture without exception. Perhaps that's what he does. Although there are great differences between the religions, there is a similar pattern. On the one hand the transcendent is posited as being totally beyond human comprehension; on the other hand, this transcendence is symbolized in images which make it intimate. The prologue of St John's gospel says that there is some light of the knowledge of God in all people in all ages: 'All that came to be was alive with his life, and that life was the light of men. The light shines on in the dark, and the darkness has never mastered it' (John 1.4–5).

Nevertheless, this knowledge of God is opaque and cloudy. Sometimes indeed, through human sinfulness, it is severely distorted. Therefore God chooses to reveal himself clearly, without distortion, in his own person. We might take the analogy of a group of musicians who admire a particular violinist. They listen to his playing on CDs and read what he has written on technique. Through this they certainly learn something. But then the great violinist comes in person and gives a master class. In the nature of things he cannot give a master class to all budding violinists: he has to choose just a few; perhaps, in some cities, only one. But through these few or this one there is a definitive disclosure of the great man's playing which is passed on to the next generation. The analogy, like all analogies, breaks down. For those who are invited to a master class have a talent which has been developed and then recognized. God chose the people of Israel and chooses Christians not because of any particular talent and certainly not because of any special merit but simply out of his free, sovereign grace. But this is not favouritism. The purpose is to share the knowledge of God as widely as possible.

It is worth exploring why we find favouritism distasteful. If a head teacher singles out a particularly attractive pupil for special treatment or one whose parents are wealthy or influential, because he wants to curry favour with them, the reason becomes apparent. But if the teacher singles out a child from a particular deprived background for a special task, in order to build up that child's confidence, then we recognize that kind of singling out is not only not unfair, it is positively to be desired. So whatever truth there is in the criticism that God has favourites, it isn't a problem of selecting the wealthy or influential. God did not choose the Chinese, the most ancient civilized race in the world, in order to give the definitive disclosure of himself. He did not choose the Greeks, whose philosophical tradition has enlightened the whole of humanity. He did not choose the Romans, whose accomplishments of law and administration laid the foundations for European civilization. He chose a small, relatively powerless tribe sandwiched between the great empires of Egypt and Syria/Babylon and later within a world dominated by the Greeks and Romans. They were people who were enslaved in Egypt and deported to Babylon; the people who lost their northern tribes to Syria and who were brutally subjugated later by the Romans.

Within Israel itself there are many examples of God choosing the least likely people, as he singled out David the shepherd to beat Goliath and who became king rather than any of his elder brothers. It is this tradition that is carried on with such poignancy and power in the New Testament. Mary, the mother of Jesus, is an unknown. The shepherds who worshipped at his birth were marginalized people. During his ministry Jesus mixed with tax collectors and prostitutes, those whom society as a whole regarded as beyond the pale. If this is favouritism it is what might now be called 'positive discrimination'. The person at the bottom of the table, in the story, is told 'Friend, go up higher.' The last shall be first and the poor are told that the kingdom of God belongs to them. In the modern world it is fundamental to liberation theology that God above all works through communities of the poor and dispossessed. They are the instruments through whom he is working in a special way to challenge the structures of economic and political justice.

Andrew Brown has written about the clerihew quoted at the beginning of this chapter that it

> . . . gains quite unintended force from any reading of the Old Testament. I suspect it was originally meant as a smooth anti-Semitic jibe, as it would have been less odd of God to choose the English. But the idea that he would choose any Bronze Age tribe is one we now find unnatural. I don't know why: people seem happy to believe that Stone Age tribes have special insights, or Silicone Age ones like ours. But the Bronze Age is completely passé outside of Kansas.

As Andrew Brown suggests, we are very happy to look for special spiritual insights in, for example, Aboriginal or Native American culture. Our hostility to Bronze Age culture comes from feminist readings of pre-history. According to this perspective human beings originally worshipped a benevolent earth goddess. It was only when men started to become dominant with their weapons that a fierce tribal God started to take charge. This is of course a gross caricature of what actually happened, though it is certainly true that early cultures were much more open to seeing the divine expressed in feminine form.

For some, the thought of such election is terrifying. Even if the criticism about favouritism is dispelled, the thought of being in the grip of an omnipotent, controlling power is both frightening and belittling of humanity. But God is not a control freak, nor is he a puppeteer. The key religious word is that of vocation, derived from the Latin word meaning call or calling. If we are called we are free to respond or not, as we choose. Nevertheless, there is something there to which we can respond if we want. Life is not an anarchic, meaningless chaos with everyone making arbitrary choices unrelated to any ultimate purpose or goal. There is an ultimate purpose. But this purpose is not imposed. We are invited first to hear and then to enter into it. Of course we fail to perceive that purpose or, worse, distort it in dangerous and destructive ways. But if love created the world, love did so in the knowledge that love would ultimately prevail. As Shakespeare put it,

> There's a divinity that shapes our ends,
> Rough-hew them how we will.[1]

For a Christian believer there is not just a general purpose for humanity as a whole, there is a particular purpose for him or her. As Cardinal Newman put it:

God has created me to do him some definite service; he has committed some work to me which he has not committed to another. I have my mission – I may never know it in this life, but I shall be told it in the next. I am a link in a chain, a bond of connection between persons. He has not created me for nought. I shall do good. I shall do his work.[2]

It is the desire and purpose of God to make himself known to all people at all times. And some knowledge of his presence and character is indeed known. But this is mediated to us through particular cultures with their particular histories. If God was going to make himself known in a more decisive and definite way, it was inevitable that he should single out one group of people which comes to a focus and climax in one person. But this knowledge of God in Jesus Christ is not meant to be the preserve of a few. The whole purpose of light breaking through at this point is that it might illuminate every single corner of the universe. It is through entering into dialogue with other religions that Christians both find themselves learning from the insights of those religions and sharing the light of the knowledge of the glory of God in the face of Jesus Christ.

CHAPTER 7

What About Good People Who Are Not Christians?

I was still in the bonds of my own Evangelical faith; and, in 1858, it was with me, Protestantism or nothing: the crisis of the whole turn of my thoughts being one Sunday morning, at Turin, when, from Veronese's Queen of Sheba, and under quite overwhelmed sense of his God-given power, I went away to a Waldensian chapel where a little squeaking idiot was preaching to an audience of 17 old women and three louts, that they were the only children of God in Turin; and that all the people in the world out of sight of Monte Viso, would be damned. I came out of the chapel, in sum of 20 years of thought, a conclusively *un*-converted man.

(John Ruskin, *Fors Clavigera*, April 1877)[1]

John Ruskin was not only one of the most admired and famous figures in the nineteenth century, he also had one of the most naturally religious minds. He had a wonderful capacity to appreciate and admire, together with a willingness to be emotionally moved by what he saw. It was this combination of gifts which made his descriptions of paintings and nature so eloquent. Charlotte Brontë wrote to a friend about Ruskin:

Who can read these glowing descriptions of Turner's works without longing to see them? . . . I like this author's style much; there is both energy and beauty in it. I like himself, too, because he is such a hearty admirer. He does not give himself half-measure of praise or vitupera-tion. He eulogises, he reverences with his whole soul.[2]

It is this ability to appreciate and admire, in such contrast to the dismissive cynicism of our own age, that finds its fulfilment in religious faith. Indeed, without it, faith is impossible. It was this capacity which gave an almost religious quality to some of Ruskin's writings.

To this we must add something which is, to our taste, something less admirable, his later belief in spiritualism. When his orthodox Christian faith waned it was replaced, as it was for a good number of other Victorians, by spiritualism. Ruskin had a lifelong, obsessive relationship with Rose La Touche. When she died comparatively young, Ruskin claimed to be able to communicate with her and, in his periods of breakdown, to see her.

To this we could also add the fact that he was brought up by parents who doted on him, who lived for him, and who were devoutly Christian. So also was Rose La Touche. So as far as religion is concerned, he could be said to have had everything going for him, for he had a naturally religious mind, with the people he most loved and admired urging him at every turn to be faithful to the Protestant understanding of Christianity. Yet, as the quotation at the head of this chapter shows, he turned against it in a most violent manner. Even allowing for the exaggeration in this passage (for in fact Ruskin went on wrestling with religion for the rest of his days), it was clearly a decisive turning-point. And although it might be argued that Protestantism is, for the most part, a great deal less narrow than it was in Ruskin's day, two points that emerge from Ruskin's reaction are still intensely relevant. What he called his un-conversion was a response to two features which many people still feel strongly about today.

First, Ruskin had just been deeply moved by a painting of Veronese and was quite overwhelmed by his sense of the artist's God-given power. In contrast, what went on in the Protestant chapel struck him as unbearable, a little squeaking idiot preaching to an audience of 17 old women and three louts.

Second, as if that was not bad enough, this group of people believed that they were the only children of God in Turin and that everybody else in the world who did not share their vision would be damned. Ruskin was filled with a sense of outrage and moral revulsion at such a view.

With the decline in formal religious belief, even more people today than in Ruskin's time find spiritual sustenance and meaning through the arts, particularly music. Unless the Christian faith can have some proper understanding and affirmation of this, it will exclude many people's most meaningful and powerful experiences. I believe that the Christian faith does offer this: for all art depends on form. Forms change, but without structure, symmetry and balance there is no art. At the same time, if this were all that art is, there would be no difference between wallpaper and a great painting, or a jingle and a symphony. Genuine art also grapples, in some way appropriate to itself, with the truth of things, and this truth has a strong moral dimension. This does not mean that works of art can become an independent source of knowledge of God. God has made himself known to us in the life, death and resurrection of Jesus Christ. But on that basis it is possible to see in works of art the imprint of the eternal logos, or word, who creates structure, order and pattern in every aspect of the cosmos – work which is reflected in the arts. To put it in a very shorthand way, the re-ordering and re-creation of the universe, even if in its most bleak and dire aspects, through the crucifixion and resurrection of Christ, has an analogue in the way that artists can take some of the most terrible experiences of human existence and, without denying their terror, create a work of art. This is not the place to develop these themes, which I have done elsewhere.[3] So I turn to the second feature of Ruskin's un-conversion. We may have some hesitation over Ruskin's exasperated sense of superiority over what he called 17 old women and three louts. After all, he was the only son of an enormously wealthy father who indulged his every whim and was a person of enormous gifts and great opportunities to use them. But that said, his repugnance at a small group of people claiming to be the saved will be widely shared.

Traditional Christianity has been extraordinarily reluctant to acknowledge the presence of genuine goodness in people of other religions or of no religion at all. I believe we should not only recognize but rejoice in such goodness: not reluctantly or begrudgingly, but gladly and gratefully. In order that this point may not remain the realm of abstraction, I will give some specific examples.

First, someone known to my wife and myself, sadly now dead. He was a consultant paediatrician who gave himself unstintingly to his work with young children. Although he knew he had a heart problem, for which he had received major treatment, he still worked long hours for his patients. He was unfailingly cheerful and encouraging, always concerned about the health of others rather than his own. His outstanding skills and qualities meant that he became a consultant at a young age: and he died young. Tesse, for that was how we knew him, came from Nigeria, and he was a devout Muslim. Even in the busiest periods in hospital he kept Ramadan, not eating from sunrise to sunset. Tesse was a wonderfully good person. That goodness had been shaped and nourished by his Muslim faith.

My second example is anonymous. I am thinking of those six million Jews who were exterminated in concentration camps during the Second World War, many of whom kept faith and hope alive despite the unspeakably barbarous and evil thing that was happening to them and all those they loved. Even on the wagons going to the camps and within the camps, amidst appalling degradation, there were those who said their prayers, acted in kindness and looked to God. The Chief Rabbi, Dr Jonathan Sacks, sums up this noble tradition of Judaism in the following words:

Over one who uninterruptedly studies God's word, said the rabbis, even the Angel of Death can win no victory. How true this was of the pious Jews of Auschwitz and Treblinka and Bergen-Belsen, discovering as they did that in the face of ultimate evil, the word of God was not silent. It had an awe-inspiring resonance. God did not die at Auschwitz, they said. He wept tears for his people as they blessed His name at the gates of death. Their bodies were given as burnt offerings and their lives as a sanctification of God's name. 'The fire which destroys our bodies', said Rabbi Elchanan Wasserman, before he was killed, 'It is the fire which will restore the Jewish people.' And so it was. The Jews of faith, who were able to sanctify death *in* the Holocaust, turned out to be the most determined to sanctify life *after* the Holocaust.

And the stubborn people have shown its obstinacy again. Faced with destruction, it has chosen survival. Lo amut ki echyeh, says the psalm: 'I will not die, but I will live', and in this response there is a kind of courage which rises beyond theology's reach . . . So with the Jewish people. Without answers, it has re-affirmed its covenant with history. The people Israel lives and still bears witness to the living God.[4]

If this is not witness to the true God, I do not know what is.

My next example is a household name, Aung San Suu Kyi, the Burmese opposition leader. Aung San Suu Kyi chose to go back to Burma to be with her people, leaving her family in the safety of Britain, even though she knew she would be arrested. She was, and until very recently has been confined to her own house. In Burma there has been a terrible abuse of human rights, with whole peoples suffering badly. Aung San Suu Kyi has become a symbol, both in her own country and in the world as a whole, for her non-violent opposition to Burma's oppressive regime. She has been totally brave, standing unarmed before guns and tanks, and morally uncompromising. Buddhism is the basis of her personal life and her political resistance. She rises at 4.30 a.m. for an hour's meditation, learns the Sutras by heart, and talks quite naturally and unselfconsciously about Buddhism when interviewed about her role in the political struggle.

What Buddhism gives her, above all, is freedom from fear. She regards fear as the emotion most likely to corrupt us. Buddhist discipline helps her to overcome fear and allows Metta, or loving kindness, to grow within her. Free from fear she is able to pursue the truth fearlessly and objectively. Furthermore, it enables her to see the good, human qualities in her captors and live free of resentment, bitterness and anger: though she does confess that she is less than perfect as far as these emotions are concerned. She is non-judgemental about others, ordinary people with ordinary human ambitions, and those who take the path of violence to achieve political liberation in Burma, as opposed to her own way of non-violence. Although we in the West see her primarily as a political figure, she herself is quite clear that religious truth and spiritual discipline, though they have to be expressed politically, are prior to and more fundamental than political action. It is her moral luminosity that comes across, and it is this which she affirms must be the basis of any viable political system. So she is fond of quoting a Buddhist verse:

> The shade of a tree is cool indeed.
> The shade of parents is cooler.
> The shade of teachers is cooler still.
> The shade of a ruler is yet more cool.
> But coolest of all is the shade of the Buddha's teaching.[5]

Although it is Buddhism which is the mainspring of her life, there have been other important influences as well. One of them is Christianity, and she is very fond of quoting a verse from the New Testament: 'Perfect love casts out fear' (1 John 4.18).[6]

She has also, I suspect, been unconsciously influenced by the political activism of the modern world. For although she is a Buddhist, she makes it quite clear that the doctrine of Karma does not simply mean letting things happen, as though they were fated – the stereotype of Buddhism in the West. On the contrary, Karma means actively taking responsibility for one's actions now and trying to change the world for the better.

Then there is the crucial influence of her father, a post-war hero in Burmese society, who was assassinated. This reminds us that all religious, philosophical and moral teaching has in the end to be embedded in and filtered through human people, and the decisive influence for most of us is our family.

More generally, the example of Aung San Suu Kyi brings out the fact that very often it is not one influence, however dominant, but a series of influences which shapes our moral outlook. For although Buddhism is central for her, her understanding of Buddhism has been shaped by the threefold influence of Christianity, modern political activism and the example of her father. It reminds us that all religious traditions have to be interpreted and there can be a range of considerations that influence this interpretation.

My next example is someone from a Hindu background, Rabindranath Tagore. Tagore was a representative of the highly sophisticated, high culture of Bengal. He was active in the struggle for Indian independence and founded a university. But he was also a poet and artist of distinction, as well as being a religious thinker of beautiful insights. He worked with Gandhi, though taking a different view from him on a number of issues, and for much of his life was better known. He and the English Socialist,

Beatrice Webb, had little in common; nevertheless she wrote about Tagore:

> He has perfect manners and he is a person of great intellect, distinction, and outstanding personal charm. He is beautiful to look at . . . Unwittingly one's practical imagination sees a great pageant, staged without limit of cost at Delhi with Tagore the magnificent saint, standing in the centre in statuesque stillness, personifying immortal India, a poor little ugly Lloyd George in shabby khaki, furtively shifting about in a far off corner, representing Western de-throned civilisation.[7]

Tagore belonged to a Reformist tradition of Hinduism, which sought to emphasize monotheism and was opposed to idolatry. Tagore's poems, sayings and stories, known as *Gitanjali*, published in an English translation before the First World War, were widely admired. The poet W. B. Yeats carried the manuscript about with him wherever he went, reading it in trains, buses and restaurants. The last words of the poet Wilfred Owen to his mother as he went off to France for the last time were words of Tagore: 'When I go from hence, let this be my passing word, that which I have seen is unsurpassable.' When Gandhi was in prison and eventually agreed to break his fast, Tagore was asked to sing him one of his Bengali songs. Gandhi's favourite was one from Tagore's *Gitanjali*: 'When the heart is hard and parched up come upon me with a shower of mercy.'

I use Tagore as an example, not only because he illustrates the moral and spiritual richness that can come from the Hindu tradition, but because he showed how religious insights from a non-Christian tradition can illuminate and nourish the spiritual journey of us all. There are innumerable examples of these in Tagore's writing. But as he saw himself not only as a poet and artist but, above all, as a musician, I quote some words on this theme that he addresses to God:

> I know not how thou singest, my master! I ever listen in silent amazement.
> The light of thy music illumines the world. The life-breath of thy music runs from sky to sky.
> The holy stream of thy music breaks through all stony obstacles and rushes on.
> My heart longs to join in thy song, but vainly struggles for the voice.
> I would speak, but speech breaks not into song and I cry out baffled.
> Ah, thou has made my heart captive in the endless message of thy music, my master![8]

My last example is Nelson Mandela: a man who has become one of the most admired people in the world. The way he survived years of prison without bitterness and then came to lead the ANC and then the new South Africa in such a constructive way has been truly remarkable. What sustained him all those years in prison and enabled him to take South Africa into a new future with so little harping on past evils? There is still a story to be told in answer to those questions, for Nelson Mandela has been characteristically reticent about this side of his life.

Anthony Sampson, who has written on Mandela, has suggested that he is an agnostic. The evidence is against this, for when in prison on Robben Island he used to receive Communion from the Methodist pastor who visited. I raised this question with the distinguished South African editor Donald Woods, foe of apartheid and friend of Steve Biko, and he shared my scepticism about Anthony Sampson's reading of Mandela's personal beliefs.

Nelson Mandela's mother was a Christian and there was certainly a period in his early life when he had to go to church regularly. He has had Christian friends and South Africa is a profoundly religious country in the way that Britain is not. There has undoubtedly been some Christian influence, but I do not believe it is the major one. Here I agree with Anthony Sampson in suggesting that this has been and continues to be the moral ideal of an African chieftain. Nelson Mandela's own father died young, and he was brought up by a chieftain, and was able to observe his style of leadership at close quarters. Mandela has said that he hugely admires this tradition of African heroes. Above all, it has conveyed what is so obvious about Nelson Mandela – his dignity. Not, of course, dignity in the sense of standing on his dignity; but what we might call a natural dignity, except that it is not so much a quality one is born with, as one which is shaped by a particular cultural tradition. The cultural tradition which has been decisive in shaping Nelson Mandela has been that of African rulers and the moral ideal associated with that kind of rule.[9]

There is also Communist idealism. Although Communism in power became tyrannical, many young people in the early and middle years of the last century were caught up in it as the best expression of their ideal of a better world. Nelson Mandela tells the story of how, when he was a young clerk, someone about his age gave him a sandwich at lunchtime and between them they pulled the sandwich roughly in half. The friend said, 'Now, eat, Nelson, what we have just done symbolizes the philosophy of the Communist Party, to share everything we have.' So again we have a range of influences – the Communist ideal and Christianity – though it is, I believe, the African tradition of leadership that has been most powerful in shaping Nelson Mandela, and in him we see qualities that people of all religious traditions and none can recognize as admirable; that is, as qualities we would like, in our best moments, to have ourselves.

So here are examples of goodness, Muslim, Jewish, Buddhist, Hindu, secular and African. Traditionally, Christianity has taken a negative attitude to goodness that has been formed and nurtured outside its own tradition, for it has emphasized that humanity is a fallen race, that we are all caught up in sin and our only hope is Christ our Saviour. Therefore, all examples of goodness are only apparent, the motivation will be flawed; especially in Protestant circles, it will be suggested that these apparently good qualities and deeds are nothing other than an attempt to justify ourselves. Now it is certainly true that something has gone fundamentally wrong with human life, and no doubt the motives of people like Aung San Suu Kyi and Nelson Mandela are as mixed as any of ours are. Moreover, they would be the first to admit that they are not perfect. Nevertheless, it seems perverse and warped not to acknowledge gladly that we see in such examples wonderful moral qualities which we would be only too glad to have for ourselves.

At this point it might be argued that the examples I have adduced concern morality, not religion. While it might be possible for people to develop genuine moral qualities, this is very different from being able to know God. I would question that in two respects. First, as already pointed out above, the qualities we admire in people like Aung San Suu Kyi or those Holocaust victims who remained faithful, was undoubtedly shaped, nourished and inspired by their religious beliefs. Furthermore, the Bible seems to make it quite clear that knowing God and acting with justice and mercy, though not identical, are integrally related. Morality and religion are not the same thing; nevertheless the Hebrew prophets suggest that those who claim to know God but who act oppressively do not in fact know him, while Jesus suggests that those who meet the needs of others are in fact serving him, whether they realize it or not (Matthew 25).

This said, there does remain a debate about the relationship between Christianity and other religions, with three main positions being taken up: the exclusivist, the pluralist and the inclusive.

The exclusivist view claims that knowledge of God is given only in and through Jesus Christ. Where Jesus Christ is not proclaimed and believed, there is no knowledge of the one true God. Christianity is the exclusive vehicle of truth. This hardly seems to be a New Testament view. In his letter to the Romans, Paul wrote:

For all that may be known of God by men lies plain before their eyes; indeed God himself has disclosed it to them. His invisible attributes, that is to say his everlasting power and deity, have been visible, ever since the world began, to the eye of reason, in the things he has made. (Romans 1.19, 20)

Paul goes on to say that people have turned away from God and this is obvious in their manner of life. Nevertheless he does presume that God can be known by those who reflect on the world he has made. Then, according to the account in the Acts of the Apostles, when Paul preached in Athens, he referred to human beings in the following words:

> They were to seek God, and, it might be, touch and find him; though indeed he is not far from each one of us, for in him we live and move, in him we exist; as some of your own poets have said, 'We are also his offspring.' (Acts 17.27, 28)

From a theological standpoint, it is difficult to see how the God who has made known his love for us in Jesus Christ and who seeks to gather to himself even those who have put themselves at a great distance from him, could have left the vast majority of human beings without any knowledge of him at all. Even if we assume that human minds are darkened by sin, and light filters through only as to the depth of the ocean, yet the God and father of our Lord Jesus Christ works unceasingly to make himself known in and through the things he has made and in and through those he has inspired in every culture. It is inconceivable that none of this knowledge gets through. So the exclusivist position must be firmly rejected. Behind it however there is an important point which will be taken up later.

The pluralist position can either be based upon an agnosticism about achieving any agreed religious truth or on an assumption that the different religions of the world are simply different routes to the one truth. Neither are satisfactory. No Christian can be indifferent to the truth. Whatever the difficulties and disagreements, we need to struggle away intellectually and theologically. The problem with thinking that the different religions of the world are but different aspects of the one truth is that there are incompatibilities between the different religious outlooks, as well as some common ground. Christianity teaches that Jesus Christ is the definitive disclosure of God. Judaism and Islam deny this. Judaism, Christianity and Islam teach that there is one God, Creator of heaven and earth, before whom in the end all will come. There is no comparable belief in Buddhism, nor in many traditions of Hinduism. To assume that there is one truth to which all the different religions point is to assume what in fact the different religions strongly disagree about. If we posit that one truth, it will be a truth conceived in terms of our own religious tradition, but other religious traditions will conceive it differently. Nor can we say that there is one truth beyond all present religions because we have no access to that truth. The pluralist position must therefore also be rejected.

The inclusivist view suggests that Jesus Christ is present in the hearts and minds of faithful people in other religions in an anonymous way.

Though not consciously believed in or proclaimed, nevertheless he is there. Christianity brings his presence into full consciousness and does so in such a way that the religious insights of non-Christian religions find their natural fulfilment in Christianity. Christianity, as it were, includes their insights, which it seeks to bring out and fulfil in itself. Attractive though this point of view is, it is open to the charge of linguistic imperialism. It means interpreting other religions in exclusively Christian terms, in fact colonizing them. So although the inclusivist view has some truth, by itself it is inadequate.

In view of the deficiencies of these three well-known positions, it seems better to avoid some great general abstraction at the beginning and, instead, concentrate on the way of dialogue. The 1988 Lambeth Conference, the great gathering of Anglican bishops from around the world, suggested that dialogue had three main features.[10] First, the attempt to understand the other person's religion in their terms. Instead of stereotyping them or projecting upon them assumptions which are alien, it is important to let other people speak for themselves and define themselves in their own terms. This kind of understanding is basic to any genuine dialogue. Second, it is possible to explore common ground and affirm this. Even between religions that appear polar opposites, say Islam and Zen Buddhism, it is in fact possible to find some truths which are asserted in common. Third, there should be a frank recognition and exploration of the differences. Genuine dialogue does not mean leaving one's most deeply held convictions behind as a precondition of discussion. On the contrary, genuine dialogue can only occur when those convictions are brought into the relationship.

There can be no agreed inter-faith goal for dialogue. Each religious participant will have a different understanding of its *raison d'être* and possible outcome. To suggest that there is one overall goal for inter-faith dialogue is to make the same mistake as the pluralist position indicated above, namely that there is some agreed truth over and above the religions of the world as they actually exist. Nevertheless, there can be a Christian goal of inter-faith dialogue. If, as is argued later, God has acted to reconstitute human society around Jesus, it is possible to look for analogies to this society, or marks of it in what other religions are trying to achieve. To put it in more traditional terms, Jesus came proclaiming the rule of God in human affairs and inviting people to live under that rule in his kingdom. In a series of vivid pictures he sketches out the kind of person who will feel at home in this world and invites people to enter it. It would be possible to explore what kind of community the dialogue partner is in fact trying to create, as well as the teaching that lies behind what it is doing. There might even be practical co-operation in trying to achieve a society with particular kinds of characteristics.

Second, from a Christian point of view, there will be an opening of the eyes and heart to see something of Christ in the other. Rowan Williams has written that, 'In theological terms, human history is the story of the discovery or realisation of Jesus Christ in the faces of all women and men.'[11]

Austin Farrer once wrote:

> Faith perishes if it is walled in or confined. If it is anywhere, it must be everywhere, like God himself: if God is in your life, he is in all things, for he is God. You must be able to spread the area of your recognition for him and the basis of your conviction about him, as widely as your thought will range.[12]

This is an important paragraph. It is not suggesting that we can find a basis for the knowledge of God independently of the Christian tradition. It does suggest that we must be able to spread the area of our recognition for Jesus and the basis of our conviction about him as widely as our thought will range. Our thought will certainly range as widely as other religions, exploring their place within the providence of God and what Christ is doing in and through them.

I suggested above in the discussion of the exclusivist view that there is one aspect of it we need to take fully into account. It is this. In the synoptic gospels (Matthew, Mark and Luke) the picture we have of Jesus is one who presents his contemporaries with a challenge, indeed a crisis of judgement: namely the presence of the kingdom. God's rule in human affairs was dramatically shown in the casting out of demons, the healing of people who were sick and in the summons to live differently. In St John's gospel the challenge is no longer that of the kingdom of God but Jesus Christ himself, in whom and through whom God's rule on earth has been inaugurated. The choice to be made now is for him or against him. To put it in terms which are discussed later, God's work is the reconstitution of human society, not just in general but in relation to and around Jesus Christ who gives himself to us as sheer gift. Rooted and grounded in him this new society, this recreation, this new humanity, is to live only in love.

There is no avoiding what has been called the scandal of particularity, the clear choice presented by Jesus himself and his ministry and by the Church about Jesus Christ. But this truth, like all religious truths, can be used to inculcate humility in oneself or a sense of superiority over others. For most of human history, sadly, religion has been used as a weapon to assert superiority over others. But the challenge presented by the action of God in Jesus Christ is primarily to oneself. His is the light before whom we are to live. That light will indeed in the end illuminate and reveal all things. But for now it should lead first to penitence for oneself and, second, thanksgiving for all that is good and of Christ in others. Rowan Williams has written:

> Can we so *rediscover* our own foundational story in the acts and hopes of others that we ourselves are re-converted and are also able to bring those acts and hopes in relation with Christ for their fulfilment by the recreating grace of God.[13]

This means, first of all, seeing something of the face of Christ in others and letting this, as Williams puts it, re-convert us. It also means bringing what is good in the other in relation to Christ. This is done first and foremost in prayers of thanksgiving.

Austin Farrer tells how, as an undergraduate, he had a friend who committed suicide. It made him realize afterwards that his desire for his friend to be converted to the Christian faith had perhaps put a barrier between them. He should instead, he thought, have thanked God for all the good qualities in his friend, and this would have broken down any barriers like nothing else. If we can open our minds and hearts to other religions and see something of Christ in them, then the proper expression of this is thankfulness to God.

One of the truths rediscovered by postmodernism is that we are all embedded in a particular culture and shaped by a particular language. We live in and through the language of our cultural tradition, which includes the religion of that culture. We have no bird's-eye point of view hovering above the different religions and judging between them. Nor should we look for what has been termed a premature closure of the story of God's developing relationship with his world. This does not mean sacrificing Christian truths. On the contrary, we live before and in him who has made God definitively accessible to us. Furthermore, we believe that he is the light in whom, in the end, all things will be seen. But meanwhile history continues with its multiple interactions, changes and, under God, transfigurations. The new relationship being established between the different religions of the world, the many forms of inter-faith dialogue now taking place, are all part of that unfolding and developing history. We cannot predict the outcome, nor should we seek to do so. Insofar as we can discern something of the face of Christ in the partners of these dialogues, Christ will call us to deepen our faith and live more faithfully to him. Insofar as we discern the face of Christ, then that is cause for profound thankfulness. Through dialogue God changes us. He also changes others.

CHAPTER 8

Why the Cruelty and Horror In Nature?

Who trusted God was love indeed
And love creation's final law –
Tho' Nature, red in tooth and claw
With ravine, shriek'd against his creed.

(Tennyson, *In Memoriam*, LV)

Without losing lucidity, indeed with added lucidity, we need to reclaim for real science that style of awed wonder that moved mystics like Blake.

(Richard Dawkins)[1]

The nineteenth century saw a series of great set-piece battles of science and religion. First, archaeological discoveries cast serious doubts upon a literalistic view of the book of Genesis. Then Darwin's theory of evolution showed that animals and human beings had evolved over a very long period of time, lower forms of life gradually evolving into higher ones and human beings being part of this process. Although 'Creationism' as it is called (that is a literalistic reading of the account of creation as we have it in Genesis) is still put forward in some fundamentalist circles, particularly in the United States of America, and although school and university debating societies still like to mount debates on the alleged clash between science and religion, the reality is very different. For historians of science are agreed that what is remarkable about the cultural history of the last half of Queen Victoria's reign was how quickly the theory of evolution was accepted, particularly by church people. Frederick Temple (1821–1902), who became Archbishop of Canterbury, pointed out in a memorable phrase that God does not just make the world, he does something more wonderful: 'He makes the world make itself.'

That said, it is true that there are some people, like my friend Richard

Dawkins, who believe that a scientific account of evolution rules out the possibility of a Creator God undergirding and guiding the whole process. Indeed, his assumption that religion offers a rival explanation to his account pops up in many of his writings. Richard Dawkins is a wonderful writer on science and has enlarged the appreciation of us all when it comes to how evolution works. I also accept and totally respect that he is an atheist. What I strongly dispute are the grounds of his atheism.

First, it is worthy of note that Charles Darwin himself did not lose his faith (indeed, he never entirely lost it) because of the theory of evolution as such. He started his scientific life as a devout Christian believer and his great mentor at Cambridge was a scientist who was also ordained. But gradually his faith was eaten away. The reason for this was the apparent waste and cruelty of nature; not the fact that we human beings have evolved from less complex species over millions of years, but the character or quality of that process undermined his faith. It was this that Tennyson referred to in the quotation above. Nature seemed nothing but predatory competition; it was red in tooth and claw and it seemed very difficult to reconcile this with a God of love behind it all.

As I hope this book shows, I take the case against religious belief with the utmost seriousness. But I find it impossible to accept that a scientific explanation of a process in itself rules out a complementary understanding which puts that process in a wider perspective. Indeed, as I am always tempted to say to Richard Dawkins, and I think I have said, 'Richard, there are enough good reasons against religion without dragging science into it.'

Opinion polls reveal that the percentage of Christian believers among scientists is the same, or even higher, than the percentage of Christian believers in the country as a whole. Certainly a good percentage of those I interview with a view to ordination have degrees in science, some of them with Doctorates as well. In fact, the real scepticism today tends to come not from science but from the arts and has to do with a range of postmodern questions which cast doubt upon our ability to establish any abiding and universal truth. As far as science and religion is concerned there has been a whole range of excellent writing from distinguished scientists who are also theologically trained, bringing the two perspectives together in a creative way which enhances one's understanding of the way God works in relation to his creation.[2] The general rule, established many years ago, still remains valid.

Scientists *qua* scientists are seeking to answer 'How' questions – how do things work, what is the process? Philosophers, theologians and all of us when we are not actually doing scientific work, address 'Why' questions: why is anything here at all and is there any ultimate purpose to the universe for us to recognize? This is not to claim that there is necessarily any answer to those 'Why' questions, certainly not that there is any agreed answer.

It may even be that the answer is no, that there is no ultimate rationale or purpose behind the universe. But in giving that answer, whether it is no or yes, we are doing something different from giving a scientific explanation. Richard Dawkins has written, 'If I ask an engineer how a steam engine works, I have a pretty fair idea of the general kind of answer that would satisfy me.' He then goes on to give a helpful understanding which relates to what he seeks to do in giving an explanation of how the process of evolution works. 'The behaviour of a complicated thing should be explained in terms of interactions between its component parts, considered as successive layers of an orderly hierarchy.'[3] He then indicates the theme of his book, namely that the amazingly complex beings, which are ourselves, have come about as a result of 'cumulative selection'. But in the same way that we can ask about an engine, 'Who invented it and for what purpose?' we can ask about creation, including the whole process of evolution, 'Does a rational purpose lie behind it and if so what is this?' Again, I would stress, there is a range of answers to those questions and we may conclude either that it is not possible to give an answer or that the answer is definitely no. But there is a non-scientific question here that a scientist might reflect on when she or he comes home in the evening; and answering that question involves taking into account not only what goes on in the laboratory but a great deal else in human life as well, even including our capacity to puzzle away at such questions.

Not long ago I took part in a public debate with Lord Winston on the ethical implications of genetics. Afterwards there was a panel comprised of a number of distinguished scientists and historians of science. I was surprised, though gratified, how nearly all of them, quite spontaneously, asserted that there is a whole range of questions that science *qua* science cannot answer.

Another distinguished scientist and writer on scientific matters, Professor Steve Jones, is not himself, I think, a believer, but has nevertheless written:

> Science cannot answer the questions philosphers – or children – ask: why are we here, what is the point of being alive, how ought we to behave? Genetics has almost nothing to say about what makes people more than just machines driven by biology, about what makes us human . . . In its early days, human genetics suffered greatly from its high opinion of itself. It failed to understand its own limits.[4]

Despite all this and despite the fact that this kind of point has been made so often, there remains a lingering suspicion in the public mind that religion and science are somehow at odds with one another. They are not, but it prompts the question as to why this myth should persist. I suspect it persists because there are some questions underlying the alleged debate which are not so often acknowledged and addressed.

One of these concerns the extraordinary success of the scientific method and its application in technology. The success of science and technology over the last 150 years has been quite staggering, whether one thinks of the exploration of space, the advances in medical research or information technology. Furthermore, it all continues apace. All this presents a very sharp contrast with religion. There are no generally agreed religious truths, religions are still prone to be antagonistic to one another; some religion is sheer bunk yet people believe it passionately, some religion is highly dangerous and damaging. Moreover, all religions seem stuck in an ancient world capable of adapting, if at all, only slowly to the world in which we now live. It is the success of scientific method and the abject failures of religion which, as much as anything, make people think that science is replacing and should simply replace a religious view of life.

All this should induce a certain humility in those of us who put forward the claims of religious truth. Let us begin by blessing God for the many achievements of modern science and the improvements it has brought about to human health and wellbeing. Let us give thanks not in a mean, niggardly or begrudging manner but wholeheartedly, fulsomely, for what the creative human mind and spirit have been able to achieve. And let us simply acknowledge that the kind of certainty which scientific method makes possible is not available in the sphere of religion. The impact of logical positivism in philosophy a few decades ago, followed by linguistic philosophy, highlighted the fact that religious assertions are in many respects different from scientific ones and cannot be either verified or falsified in any straightforward way in this life. Religious language has a different kind of logic and purpose which has its own validity. This means that this side of the coming of the kingdom, there will continue to be diversity, claim and counter-claim.

In this situation it behoves religious traditions to go back to the central, testing cores of their belief:

> He has showed you, O man, what is good;
> and what does the Lord require of you
> but to do justice, and to love kindness,
> and to walk humbly with your God?
>
> (Micah 6.8)

The theory that human beings have evolved from simpler organisms over millions of years presents no difficulty in itself to Christian belief. However, two features of evolution do tend to undermine religious faith. One is the apparently random and arbitrary nature of the whole process and the other is the fact that it all seems so cruel.

First, then, there is the apparently chance way in which evolution has come about. However, there are in fact two mechanisms involved. One of them is certainly arbitrary, namely random genetic variation. The other mechanism is natural selection. What this means, quite simply, is that species have to find a way of adapting to and surviving in their environment or they die out. There are a million million ways of surviving, whether it is by growing a long neck like a giraffe to eat the leaves on trees that other animals cannot reach (together with a fair turn of speed to get away from predators), or camouflage, so that an insect is virtually indistinct from the leaf on which it settles, or a capacity to burrow deep in the ground or hide in the depths of the ocean – and so on.

As a result of totally random genetic variations, a species develops characteristics that enable it to adapt and survive better. Those without such characteristics simply die out and therefore what was an originally random genetic variation is, as it were, captured and preserved for posterity; or at least until further variations enable it to cope in an even more sophisticated manner.

What may strike the religious mind is that this seems a very odd way for the creator of the universe to go on. We feel it would be more becoming to say 'Let there be' and then everything would arrive fully formed: or it could be more rational to let nature adhere to set patterns in accord with Einstein's view that God does not play dice with the universe. Whereas, on the contrary, random genetic mutation does appear to be simply that – playing dice over and over again.

However, further reflection reveals that it is in fact this *combination* of random variation and natural selection that enables what is genuinely new to emerge. If there were no genetic variation, and only the pressure of natural selection, species would be stuck for ever with what they originally had. Indeed it is difficult to see how evolution could have developed beyond the most rudimentary forms of life, even if it had been possible for life to evolve at all. On the other hand, if there were only random variation – and no pressure of natural selection – those variations most beneficial to the survival of the species would not be preserved. There would be endless variations but each one would simply perish. It is the combination of variation with the constant pressure provided by an environment in which the species seeks to survive that allows not only for the emergence of what is new but its preservation.

Although we see this combination in its most stark form in nature, it is in fact that combination which allows for the development of many of our own most helpful qualities. In a school, for example, there is usually pressure to succeed in one way or another. Some do this through sport, others through work. Some who may not be particularly good at either discover a talent as an actor or a woodworker. One pupil, not good at anything and always in trouble, develops a capacity to tell funny stories: that is the way he survives, that is, gets the attention and affection of his peers. It is not surprising if later in life he becomes a famous comedian.

Then, without implying an uncritical acceptance of the market economy, we can see a similar combination in the pressure of 'Make a success of your business or go bankrupt' together with innovative skills to find and meet customer needs, say in shopping over the Internet, that results in the emergence of successful new businesses. Or, to take an artistic analogy, an artist in whatever medium, whether a composer, painter or sculptor, always works with something given, some specific material such as stone or clay, or rules of musical notation. It is the combination of such fixity and human creativity that produces works of art. If one or other was not present this would not happen. So, more generally in life, we live in an environment characterized by regularity and stability; all those observed patterns in nature, on the basis of which we can make reliable predictions about the future, which we call laws of nature. But we are also, within limits (which may be very tight), free to shape the future of others and ourselves. What appears distinctive about evolution therefore is in fact entirely congruous with what we know to be essential in our life as human beings: it is what enables genuine creativity to take place. Our creativity as human beings, which is part of what we mean by being made in the image of God, brings into consciousness the creativity that runs through the length and breadth of creation.

The other feature of evolution which can be even more testing of religious faith is its apparent cruelty. And it is not just the cruelty in itself but the seemingly grotesque and horrific aspects of life that go with it.

One of the great successes of television are the nature programmes. Millions of viewers have had a superb opportunity to see nature at close quarters, whether in South American rainforests, the bottom of the sea or on some African plain. Much of what is shown is beautiful, evoking a sense of delight and wonder in life. But there are other scenes that shock and even repel: creatures eating others as they themselves are being eaten; insects being devoured by their female as they copulate. Above all there is the theme of eat and be eaten. Animal life seems to consist of an endless search for prey with an unceasing anxiety about becoming prey to others. Then there are the horrific creatures that can be discovered living in the depths of the ocean – to our eyes grotesque in their shape and colouring and evoking a sense of horror. So the question presses, this time even harder, can this really be the work of an all-wise and kindly creator? It seems just the opposite of what we mean by kindliness. Then there is the odd fact that most species that have lived on the earth have in fact already perished. Not just the dinosaurs but thousands of others had their place in the sun for a few million or a few hundred million years and then died out for ever. We wonder what the point of it all was. It is true that they provided rungs on the long ladder of evolution which eventually produced us. But all that apparent cruelty and waste seems a huge price to pay.

In response to such feelings a number of considerations can be adduced. They don't instantly solve all the problems, and one in particular remains, namely the pain of the higher vertebrates; but they can bathe the process of evolution in a softer light. First, with the exception just mentioned, most creatures that have lived and do live are not capable of feeling pain. They live and die without any consciousness that they are living or will die, without fear and without pain. The sight of an insect that is itself being eaten as it eats another horrifies us. But one point is clear and that is that this could not take place if the insect felt pain. Second, as argued in a previous chapter, creation exists for its own sake, not only as a necessary lead-in to humanity. One of the insights of the modern environmental movement is that creation is of value in itself. There are innumerable species of birds for example, but it is a sadness to us if one of them dies out. We appreciate the great richness and variety of creation for its own sake. Humanity may be the crown and climax of creation, as the fathers of the Eastern Church like to stress and as is expressed in Eucharistic Prayer G of the Church of England's *Common Worship*:

> From the beginning you have created all things
> And all your works echo the silent music of your praise.
> In the fullness of time you made us in your image,
> The crown of all creation.[5]

This does not mean that everything before humanity in evolution is simply an introduction or prelude. It exists for its own sake and as such reflects the glory of God whose nature and will is to create. A thousand thousand species may have perished with the dodo but each in its own way glints with a fragment of the glory of God.

Third, the beauty we see in nature is in fact a by-product of its basic drive to survive. In short, butterflies were not designed with our eyes in mind; their colours have come about as a way of helping them to adapt to and survive in particular kinds of environment against particular kinds of predator. The implication of this is that some of the shapes and colours which have come about as a result of evolution do not delight our eyes. What is perhaps surprising is how little in nature in fact strikes us as grotesque and how much as delightful. Furthermore, even when some creature sends a shudder through us – a snake, a spider, a slimy creature of the sea – there are those who feel a sense of awe. Snakes for example have been an important part of many religions in the world and in Coleridge's *The Rime of the Ancient Mariner* the narrator was released from his burden by seeing watersnakes in the sea:

> O happy living things! No tongue
> Their beauty might declare:
> The spring of love gushed from my heart
> And I blessed them unaware.[6]

Third, although the natural world is highly competitive, it is not lacking in qualities of co-operation and altruism.

I realize of course that to write in these terms is anthropomorphic, but that is how nature strikes us; for survival in nature does not necessarily mean killing off all one's rivals. Above all, it means being able to mate, breed and rear young successfully. Success is measured in terms of the ability of offspring to survive long enough for them to produce offspring that will survive. This in itself means that species develop qualities of nurture, care and protection. Further, within any one species there is this co-operation, but what matters is not the survival of a particular individual as such but survival of the species as a whole, and it is more likely to survive if it is co-operative. This co-operation operates at a genetic level first of all. Given all this it is possible to wonder whether the predatory element in nature has not been overstated in both books and films. One wonders whether the American model of a highly competitive free market, together with a fundamentally antagonistic view of the relationship of states on the international scene, has not influenced, for example, the way evolution is depicted on the screen – even apart from the fact the violent clashes make dramatic viewing.

The considerations so far adduced do not however solve the problem of the so-called higher animals, vertebrates with developed nervous systems. It is clear that such animals do feel pain and probably fear as well. Pain and its concomitant, fear, are of course protective devices built in by nature in order to help us survive. It is pain and the fear of pain which forces us to take the necessary precautions, and this is as true of dogs, horses and monkeys as it is of human beings. We feel pain, but as human beings we can make a conscious decision that life is worth while, that life is a blessing. The higher animals, so far as we know, cannot make this conscious decision. All we can hope is that nevertheless, for as long as they live, they feel their life to be a blessing.

The question arises as to where in the long process of evolution we can see the hand of God at work. So far in this chapter I have considered objections to seeing evolution as the work of a loving creator. But, more positively, where can the divine leading in it all be discerned?

In recent years the 'anthropic principle' has been much discussed and indeed championed by a number of scientifically trained theologians. This points out that the conditions of the universe are quite amazingly well adjusted for the emergence of first life itself and then us human beings. The slightest deviation from what we have at any point would have meant that either there would be no life at all or no human life. The universe looks as though it has been designed to lead up to us anthropoids (hence the anthropic principle – *anthropos* is of course Greek for man or human being).

The universe is indeed amazingly, wonderfully adapted for the production of human life: but this sense of wonder can be shared, as it is by people like Richard Dawkins, without it being seen as a compelling *rational* reason to believe that there is a creator behind it. I have to say that while I certainly share the sense of wonder, I have never been convinced by the anthropic principle. At an obvious level, of course, the universe is indeed finely tuned to bring about human life; but we would not be here to tell the tale unless it was. A more basic fallacy however has to do with the argument from design.

The universe certainly seems designed, and this led Archdeacon Paley in his famous argument to suggest that there must be a divine designer. If we discover a watch on the beach we think there must be a watchmaker. We see a universe of most amazing complexity, intricacy and balance and the mind leaps to the conclusion that there is a divine designer behind it all. The problem, quite simply, is that we have no agreed examples of designed and un-designed universes with which to compare this one. If I am walking through the jungle and I come across a clearing with vegetables growing in it, I assume that human beings are present, for I have a clear picture in my mind of land cultivated by human beings and land left to itself, as in the jungle. But by definition, the universe is *sui generis*, truly unique. There is only one example of it. There are no categories of designed and un-designed universes with which to compare this one. This means that we are never in a position, from a purely rational point of view, to say that the universe is either designed by a divine creator or not; the matter, from a strictly rational point of view, is totally open. That is also the reason why the argument of Richard Dawkins fails. The fact that he can set out the process of evolution in such a compelling way, from a scientific point of view, and account from a scientific point of view for every feature of evolution, tells us nothing about whether or not there is a divine creator behind the whole process. This argument also applies to the anthropic principle. For we have no examples of universes which have been designed to lead up to human beings and no examples of universes that arrived at human beings without divine help. Again, the matter is left totally open – from a strictly rational point of view.

Where then do we discern God? First of all, in our own lives, by responding to the leading of the Spirit and seeking to align our will with the will of God for our lives. As Austin Farrer wrote:

There is only one point at which we can possibly touch the nerve of God's creative action, or experience creation taking place: and that is in our own life. The believer draws his active Christian existence out of the wellspring of divine creation, he prays prayers which become the very act of God's will and his will. Because we have God under the root of our being we cannot help but acknowledge him at the root of all the world's being.[7]

A similar movement of the heart and mind takes place in relation to the process of evolution. Any divine pressure there might be leading matter to evolve into life and then for life to evolve into self-conscious life in us, is totally hidden. But the believer knows something of that pressure in his or her own life. We know the interaction of our will with a divine will. We also know that in order to create any one of us God had to create a universe. The whole universe comes to a focus in us. So in faith we believe that the same divine will has been active at every point in the evolutionary process. It may be that the believer, struck again by the complexity, wonder and beauty of the world, will find that their mind moves to acknowledge a wondrous Creator and their heart to praise him. The argument from design, as it were, traces out the journey that the heart of the believer makes and the mind finds it natural to make that journey because it already believes. It is rational for a believer to see the hand of God in evolution because he or she already knows the leading, prompting, the guiding and the illumination of the God of evolution in his or her own life, a life that has been brought about as a result of that process of evolution. Richard Dawkins has a sense of awe and wonder before the world which science uncovers. Christians share that sense of wonder but ground it, and the world to which it is a response, in the wondrous, uncreated source of wonder-full creation.

PART 3

The Case Against Religion

CHAPTER 9

Religion Is Stuck In the Past

We shall see a further decline of faith on the empirical level and of the practice of religion and the influence of the church as we have so far known it. We shall feel as though we are living among people thoroughly opaque to religion, talking to deaf ears and uncomprehending hearts . . . We have too an unpleasant sense whenever we hear the sound of our own voice that it is not particularly surprising that no one listens to us. Doesn't a great deal of what we say sound strange in our own ears – outmoded, utterly out of date?

(Karl Rahner SJ)

This experience will be echoed by anyone who has had experience of religion today. The language of the Church has gone dead, or almost dead, on us. Its images are strange, sometimes barbaric. It seems remote and sometimes even alien. This is reinforced in many ways; for example, the dress of the clergy conveys a sense of living in the past, as do the artefacts and images that can be seen in church. The seriousness of this situation has, I think, to be recognized. To begin with, it has two aspects: first, the fact that the language of religion is increasingly remote as already indicated. Second, the religion with which the language is connected is rapidly disappearing – at least in Europe – and will soon belong entirely to the past; or that, at least, is how it can seem. Every empire falls, every culture passes. What is there to make us think, we might say, that Christianity will escape this inexorable law, that everything that once had its day eventually passes?

Against this, it is important to recognize how dominated we are now by the present and how shaped our understanding of the present is by commercial forces. Our view of the world, our feel for it and our evaluation of it, is dominated by the media. What we see on television, hear on the radio and read in the newspapers and glossy magazines shapes how we feel and think. Behind all this, with the honourable exception of continually threatened public service broadcasting, are people who want to sell us things. They have a powerful vested interest in getting us to be obsessed by the present, by what is fashionable, by what we can buy now because it is advertised. Most people are sensible enough not to be totally taken in by all this. They have basic values from elsewhere – from their family or their school, from the armed forces or one of the caring professions or traditions of public service that still do exist. Yet even these can be infiltrated, eroded and shaped by commercial forces in ways that we may not fully be aware of.

In order to escape the tyranny of the present we need, quite consciously, to draw wisdom from a longer, deeper tradition. Tradition can act as a counterweight to the passing fashions that so beset us. The past is not only a source of wisdom but something against which the modern world can be assessed and perhaps judged. The Church is often criticized for being resistant to change but church tradition can counter the vacuousness of modern fads and mores; it can be a yardstick against which to judge what is good and valuable in modern society and what is not. As Clifford Longley has put it, religions are essentially conservative institutions:

> They exist to make the past present. They apply ancient teachings to the problems of today. They test everything new by old principles, in the name of which they sometimes supply a break. They agree with Edmund Burke that civilisations cannot be deconstructed and rebuilt in each generation but depend on continuity, things handed down. One of those things handed down is faith, which is foundation of all the others.

A distinction needs to be made between traditionalism and being part of a tradition. Traditionalists like to hold on to details of the tradition, just because they are old, familiar and reassuring. They hate change. People like this are found in the churches, as well as elsewhere. A priest once asked his parochial church council what they thought the purpose of the Church was. One old gentleman replied, 'To turn the clock back as far as it will go and keep it there.' In contrast to this, those who understand what tradition really is find it a continually renewing source. They don't champion the past because it is the past. They draw from the wells of past wisdom that which enables them to live wisely in the present.

One of the most notable examples of the proper use of tradition in the modern age is T. S. Eliot. Few have entered so deeply into the tradition of Europe as he did. He quite consciously immersed himself in its literature and religion. Yet he was the great innovating poet of the twentieth century, the modern of moderns, whose poetry shaped the whole literary tradition of modernism. Eliot wrote that it is vital for a poet to have a historical sense:

> The historical sense involves a perception, not only of the pastness of the past, but of its presence, the historical sense compels a man to write not only with his own generation in his bones, but with the feeling that the whole literature of Europe from Homer until today and within it the whole literature of his own country, has a simultaneous existence and composes a simultaneous order. This historical sense which is a sense of the timeless as well as the temporal and the timeless and the temporal together, is what makes a writer most acutely conscious of his place in time, of his own contemporaneity.[1]

That last sentence is of vital importance. It is through having a sense of tradition that we are most acutely aware of the present. We can see it for what it is, locate it in its place in history, rather than be befuddled and bewitched by it.

There is, however, another question, a hard one. For Christians not only accept tradition as something to draw on and use as they want; part of this tradition, the biblical part, is regarded as authoritative. There is a particular piece of history from Abraham through to Jesus and his immediate post-resurrection followers which is regarded as definitive for all times. All religions are faced with this question. They have a particular founder or series of founders to whom the religion looks back. Even Hinduism, which is probably freer of this kind of claim than other religions, has the Upanishads, writings which are regarded as authoritative and which pre-date Christianity. The question presses particularly hard upon Christianity however because of what has been called 'the scandal of particularity'. God does not just disclose his mind and purpose in a people but in a particular person, Jesus of Nazareth. The question of why God should reveal himself in a particular way, which can sometimes give rise to the charge of favouritism, was considered in an earlier chapter. The point at issue here is that because Christianity makes this claim it seems tied to particular events in a particular culture which must become ever more remote as the past recedes.

If, as Christians believe, God has chosen to give a definitive disclosure of himself in a particular person at a particular time, then this problem will never go away. But, Christians claim, it is the glory of God that he has chosen to enter into the flux of human history and change it from within. We would not have it otherwise. To pick up an analogy used earlier, a master class by a famous violinist might only have occurred once, to a small group of people. But better to have that, than only to be able to learn about that violinist's technique through the words of others.

God has indeed revealed himself quite specifically and definitively at one point in human history. And although, as a historical fact, this might belong more and more to the past, it continues to live in the present through the tradition of the Church and the ever-present vivifying power of the Holy Spirit which Jesus promised. The community of the church is a living tradition relating to the risen Christ and empowered by his Spirit. Through the resurrection of Christ his life and death have been given a universal contemporaneity. They bear upon every moment in every place. They become present as the word of God is preached and the sacraments are celebrated.

A few years ago the Cambridge theologian Don Cupitt did a series of television programmes whose basic assumption was that Christianity belongs inevitably to the past and is unbelievable today. But as the philosopher Keith Ward, who was in dialogue with Cupitt, pointed out: at the very time Cupitt was making this assertion the four major chairs in philosophy at the Universities of Oxford and Cambridge were held either by believing Christians or by people who were sympathetic to the claims made by traditional Christianity. At a more general level it has been pointed out that the percentage of religious believers among trained scientists is in proportion to believers in the population as a whole. Christianity continues to be believed in by philosophers and scientists alike. What the present context highlights is the importance of individual decision and personal faith.

The quotation at the head of this chapter by Karl Rahner, the distinguished Roman Catholic theologian, again brings out the point that the difficulties in believing are very often felt most acutely by believers themselves. Karl Rahner went on to write:

> The present crisis of belief is so to speak normal. Faith is always a miracle of election and grace . . . Nor shall we regret the return to the normal state of affairs. It enables people to see more clearly that faith is risk, decision and a personal relationship with God in Christ that obligates the individual to responsibilities going far beyond the passive reception of the general teachings and directives of the church.

People today are indeed fascinated by the past. We love to explore ancient ruins and watch television series about past civilizations or archaeological finds. Exploration of the past, like the arts, has become in some sense a substitute for religion. It is also an aspect of the secularization of our society that religious artefacts have become desacralized. People love to visit churches and see religious paintings in art galleries. Religion has, as it were, become part of the museum culture: a theme park to be trotted around with amusement and curiosity. The advantage of seeing religion as part of a museum culture is that we can stand over it, observe it and talk about it in a detached manner. We drain it of its claims and need not notice its authority. But Christianity is a living tradition. It mediates to us the eternal word of God which speaks to us now and for always. It is that living tradition that enables us to be fully present in the present. It helps us to see life in terms of what Pierre de Caussade called 'The sacrament of the present moment' and what the American theologian Paul Tillich termed 'The eternal now'. With extraordinary subtlety, richness and poetic strengths, this is the theme explored by T. S. Eliot in 'The Four Quartets'. We are inescapably part of history. But it is within history that we can hear

> The voice of the hidden waterfall
> And the children in the apple-tree
> Not known, because not looked for
> But heard, half-heard, in the stillness
> Between two waves of the sea.
> Quick now, here, now, always –
> A condition of complete simplicity
> (Costing not less than everything)
> And all shall be well and
> All manner of thing shall be well
> When the tongues of flame are in-folded
> Into the crowned knot of fire
> And the fire and the rose are one.[2]

CHAPTER 10

Religion Is Divisive

Say, was not this thy passion, to foreknow
In death's worst hour the works of Christian men?
(Algernon Swinburne)[1]

One of the commonest accusations against religion of all kinds, not just Christianity, is that it causes conflict. It divides communities from each other and fuels violence. People point to Northern Ireland, the Middle East, the Crusades and the wars of religion in Europe. There is clearly truth in this criticism. It must be acknowledged and taken with the utmost seriousness.

First of all, unscrupulous leaders can use religion to stir up hatred, and gullible people, sometimes with good motives, can easily be misled. I took part in a television programme during which the broadcaster Martin Bell told us how in Bosnia he met the notorious killer Arkan. Arkan pulled open his shirt to expose a large cross on his chest. 'See,' he said, 'I am a Christian.' Much more common than military leaders like Arkan have been politicians who have used religion to gain support for their cause. So religion is certainly associated with many conflicts even in the world today.

When it comes to history this is even more apparent. However, we need to avoid making quick, superficial judgements. Even the Crusades, which certainly should not be defended, were the result of a whole range of complex factors – economic, political and social, as well as religious. Christianity had been in retreat before the forces of Islam for more than half a millennium, access to the holy places in Palestine was being blocked and there was a stirring of a new religious idealism as well as a desire for land and booty among the younger sons of the French nobility. Even more important is the warning often made to us by historians that we should not condemn the attitudes of people in the past by standards which we accept today but which did not prevail in the same way in the past. I am grateful that our time does not romanticize military endeavour, even though it may sometimes be a tragic necessity. But for most of European history the concept of a chivalrous knight, especially one who was prepared to fight and if necessary lay down his life for the faith in countries far away, was regarded as a noble ideal. It's not our ideal but we have to recognize what it was and what it meant to, say, people in the twelfth century. At the same time this does not prevent us from acknowledging that in the light of that ideal, the Arab leader Saladin appears in a more favourable light than most of the Crusaders.

When it comes to the modern era the main role of religion in situations of conflict has been as a marker of identity. It has not itself been the cause of the conflicts.[2] For example, with the break-up of former Yugoslavia the different nations resumed their age-old quarrels. As it happened, Croatia was predominantly Roman Catholic; Serbia, Orthodox; and Bosnia, mainly Muslim. In the terrible wars that have taken place over the last decade religion has sometimes been a badge or symbol of a group's identity. But it did not initiate the wars. Sometimes we may feel that a religion has been too closely identified with the cause of its nation, not critical enough of its leaders. That is certainly a failing of religion that has often been exhibited in the past.

Sadly there are many conflicts and wars in the world today, but many of them take place without any reference to the religious dimension. The terrible killing between Hutus and Tutsis in Rwanda for example took place on tribal, rather than religious grounds. Neither Roman Catholics nor Protestants did enough to stop the killing but neither religion was a cause of the conflict, nor an accentuating factor. Similarly the Kurds are attacked by Turkey, Iraq and Syria because they are Kurds claiming the right to self-determination. Whether their religion is shared or not shared by the surrounding nations is not a factor in the struggle.

It is also important to take into account the mostly unsung good that religious people do during wars and in times of conflict. There are numerous stories of religious people courageously going beyond tribal or national boundaries. In Northern Ireland for example there have been very many heroic actions, mostly unbroadcast, by both Catholics and Protestants. These are people reaching out to the other community in acts of kindness or bravery or forgiveness. Religions provide people with an inspiring ideal. All adherents of religion make some effort, however feeble, to translate that ideal into practice, to overcome the feelings of aggression or malevolence that we human beings share. It is true that we are not nearly serious enough about this. As Jonathan Swift wrote, 'We have just enough religion to make us hate, but not enough to make us love one another.' But that is not the fault of religion as such: it is because we are not religious enough.

The sad, tragic fact is that we human beings are prone to kill one another. The Nazis who, after they had exterminated the Jews intended also to destroy Christianity, not only gassed six million Jews but were responsible for the deaths of many more millions of people of all kinds. Stalin, as a result of his ideology, was responsible for the deaths of 28 million in the great purges that took place in the 1930s in the Soviet Union. The most powerful force last century was in fact neither Communist ideology nor religion, but nationalism. It is this that lay behind the First World War. It is this which was responsible for the break-up of the old European empires. It is this which fragmented Communism and led to the break-up of the former Soviet Union. There is a parallel to be made here with religion. We find our identity, in part, through identifying with our locality and our wider communities, including our nation. It is entirely natural that we should find our identity, in part, in that kind of way. Nationalism has been horribly abused in the past and is responsible for some of the most terrible evils that the world has known. But that does not mean to say that all feelings of love for country should be eliminated or that people should stop feeling it proper to be English or French or German. What has begun to change and what needs to change even more is what it means to belong to a nation. Similarly, religion, in the ways already indicated, has to bear some responsibility for the terrible ills that have afflicted the world. But it is entirely natural and proper that religious people should come together in organized communities. What has changed and must change even more is the way people view these communities and especially the relationship between these communities and those truths to which they point. There is a particular danger in religion, one which is more fraught with the possibility of evil than even nationalism. For all religions claim to mediate the absolute. It is easy to topple over the brink and identify that absolute with the finite and fallible human structures through which that absolute is disclosed to human beings. In short, religion can reinforce religious communities and religious organizations in being impervious to criticism and thinking that their claims override all others, even basic human rights. That is the terrible temptation and abyss facing all religions, by their very nature.

It is what we mean by idolatry. Idolatry is to regard that which is less than ultimate as ultimate. Idolatry can take many forms. It happens in nationalism when we regard the nation state as the most important thing in life, overriding all other claims. But the temptation to idolatry is particularly acute in religion, because of its claim to point to the ultimate. The challenge is to point to the ultimate without identifying the human instruments which do this with the ultimate itself. Because the danger is always so great, it is vital that religions in the world today and in the future have built-in mechanisms of self-criticism. This is what Christianity means by repentance, which is not beating one's breast or trying to make oneself feel guilty for what one doesn't feel guilty about. The Greek word *metanoia* means to rethink, to rethink one's whole life in the light of God's just and gentle rule. In this sense all religions of the world need to live on the basis of a permanent repentance, a permanent built-in critique and rethinking in the light of that religion's highest ideals.

Religions by their very nature engage people passionately. By definition, if a person has a religion it will be the most important thing in their life: that by which their identity is formed and that by which they seek to live. Furthermore, if they believe their religion to be a disclosure of ultimate truth, they will want all people to share this truth. In the past, religions have sometimes thought that it was legitimate to share this truth through coercion of various kinds. We now quite rightly regard this as totally illegitimate, a denial of everything that religions stand for. But it is still true that religion will engage people passionately. This makes it even more vital that there is in every religious tradition the means of calling itself to account by its highest ideals.

Religion is playing an increasingly important role in the modern world. If fundamentalism is on the increase in some countries, so is the move towards inter-faith dialogue. There are now a good many contacts in which Jews, Muslims and Christians as well as people of the other great religions of the world come together in a spirit of honest encounter. There is a growing recognition that religion is a vital factor in the peace of the world. As Hans Küng puts it:

> There can be no on-going human society without a world ethic for the nations.
> There can be no peace among the nations without peace among the religions
> There can be no peace among the religions without dialogue between the religions.[3]

Secular humanists argue that we should find our identity not through religion, which has been a divisive factor, but through simple acknowledgement of our shared humanity. All religions have the resources within them to help their adherents do this in their own distinctive way. The great nineteenth-century Anglican theologian F. D. Maurice once wrote:

> Religions divide men from one another and tempt them to boast of what they possess and others do not. The gospel is the proclamation that they already belong together as children of the one God and Father of all.

That is to put it in Christian terms. But Judaism, Islam and the other great religions of the world are able to state the same truth in their own categories. This is not to deny the very real differences there are between religions or to make the unfounded assumption that they are all saying the same thing in different words. They are not. But there is much common ground, which is being increasingly explored; and there is that within every religion which can help its adherents both affirm their common humanity with all other human beings and live by ideals which are widely shared.

CHAPTER 11

Religion Keeps People Immature

> The attack by Christian apologetics upon the adulthood of the world I consider to be in the first place pointless, in the second ignoble and in the third un-Christian. Pointless, because it looks to me like an attempt to put a grown-up man back into adolescence, i.e. to make him dependent on things on which he is not in fact dependent any more . . . Ignoble, because this amounts to an effort to exploit the weakness of man for purposes alien to him and not freely subscribed to by him . . . The question is, Christ and the newly matured world.
>
> (Dietrich Bonhoeffer)[1]

The quotation is part of a long letter written by Dietrich Bonhoeffer in prison on 8 June 1944. In this he sketches out how from the thirteenth century human beings have been more and more able to cope with all the major problems of human existence without recourse to God. He then criticizes Christians who ignore the fact that, in a profound sense, humanity has come of age. The fact that this criticism comes from a Christian believer bears out the point made in the Introduction to this book, that Christian believers ought to be more acutely aware than others of the critique which can be made of their religion. This was certainly true of Bonhoeffer, whose letters written more than 50 years ago still reverberate in our own time.

The criticism that religion fosters immaturity has a number of different aspects to it, which tend to intertwine and reinforce one another. First is the emphasis that Christianity lays on the notion of dependence. If a 45-year-old man was still totally dependent upon his 70-year-old mother, we would talk about arrested development. In such a scenario we recognize that something has gone wrong. To grow up means, in some important sense, to become independent of one's parents, capable of living one's own life and taking responsibility for one's own decisions. If one never takes a decision without consulting one's parents, and even worse, only does what they tell us to do, then there has been a failure to grow up. Yet much Christian imagery seems to posit a similar state of immaturity in our relationship with God.

Here, once again, warning lights need to flash fiercely about the nature of religious language. The word 'dependent' needs to be written like that, in inverted commas, to alert the reader that the word is being used in a special way. Like all metaphors it may make a valid, indeed essential point; but like all metaphors it is as untrue as it is true. When we talk about dependence upon God, we are talking about dependence in the sense that we are dependent upon the ground on which we walk or the air which we breathe. We are trying to point to that radical dependence of all things on the power which moment by moment holds us in being. All things spring forth from the creative hand. To acknowledge this is not arrested development but acknowledgement of reality: and it is a mark of maturity to acknowledge reality.

This brings out another crucial point. Although believers and non-believers may share some ideals and the language in which those ideals are described, further probing and exploration may in fact indicate some fundamental differences. For example, both believers and non-believers can subscribe to the importance of human self-fulfilment, but from a Christian point of view we will need to ask questions about the self which is to be fulfilled. It is not the egocentric, grasping self but that Christ who is living and growing within us, our true self. Furthermore, like all good things, fulfilment cannot be found simply by seeking it; it comes as a by-product of seeking something else. It is when we are given over to what is worthwhile that we find our fulfilment. This has a bearing on our understanding of dependence. When a religious believer acknowledges the radical dependence of all things on the ground of being, this is maturity, not immaturity.

The other aspect of Christian morality that comes under attack is its language of command and obedience. Such language not only encourages immature dependence, it can be dangerous. It encourages people to submit to standards and values which, if they thought about, they would reject. It encourages them to obey commands which, if they reflected on seriously, they might regard as immoral. The example of Nazi Germany, in which the most terrible things happened in part because of a culture saturated by notions of command and obedience, remains a terrible warning.

In response to this serious criticism we need to 'locate' language about command and obedience. It arises first of all because of the claims which certain moral values and ethical ideals make upon us. There are certain actions which are simply wrong, whatever the cost or consequences. It is wrong to torture other people. It is wrong to kill babies. Such judgements are not simply a matter of taste, as when you say that you like strawberry ice cream and I say that I like chocolate. It would be grotesque to say 'You like helping people and I like torturing them' as though this settles the ethical dispute. In short, values are not simply a human invention or construct: they are recognized and responded to. The moral dimension is there to be discovered and explored. It makes a claim upon us. Although it is certainly true that standards can vary from culture to culture and age to age, and in our time many fixed points are being moved, there yet remain certain fundamentals. For example, two young people might reject the church's teaching that full sexual intercourse has its proper place only within marriage. But they might have very high standards about the respect which is due to the other person, about the importance of consent. Unless they were being wilfully perverse, they would not say that the importance of respect and free consent are simply matters of taste or human preference. They are values which claim us and call for our assent.

It is this sense of claim associated with moral values that is at the heart of language about command. But one further step is needed. This sense of claim is ultimately rooted in the being and purpose of God. He is the source and standard of all values. So when a scientist is struggling to be absolutely truthful in the experiments she is carrying out or when a writer is struggling to express himself with total integrity or when a business person is true to their word, the values inherent and expressed in such ways have their origin in God who is truth and who enjoins us to follow truth.

Then there is a further aspect. In our relationships with other human beings what they want of us is very closely related to the kind of person they are. For example, if both parents are musical then it is not surprising that they want their children to develop all the musical potential that they have within them. If they are deeply caring people, it is not surprising that they want their children to grow up caring. In such relationships we can very often experience what they want of us as a pressure; not an oppressive one but something which distinguishes their attitude from indifference. To go to the other extreme, if a person's whole life centres around the pub, it may be that all they ask of a friend is that they be a good drinking companion. They ask no more. If God is perfect love, given over to the wellbeing of his children, then it is an essential aspect of that love that he wants us also to grow in love. We feel what he wants of us as a pressure.

We have not only a good example but a definitive expression of this truth in the New Testament. There we have a picture of Jesus living his life totally given over to others. In his teaching and the way he lived, culminating in his death, his is a life for others which reveals God's unconditional love. At the same time, Jesus put before people the highest possible standards. He set before us the absolute values of the kingdom of God. We are to forgive one another not just seven times but 70 times seven.

We are not only to get on with those who are congenial to us, we are actively to love those who are hostile, and so on. His ethic was not a prudential ethic, not an ethic of nicely calculated less and more. It has a total, haunting claim about it. So we have two sides of the same coin. On the one hand God's unconditional love for his creatures, and on the other side the call and claim that we ourselves are to grow in this kind of love.

A language of command is therefore located first of all in the sense of claim which all moral values make upon us. We trace this claim back to the being and purpose of God. God, who has disclosed himself to us in Jesus, shows a boundless generosity towards us and at the same time invites us to share in that generosity and so become more and more like him. It is this that gives rise to the image of 'command'.

Obedience is the response to this. It is certainly not a question of reading some rule book and then putting the rule into practice. In many situations a great deal of thought is required, as well as agonizing about what exactly is the right course of action in the complex circumstances with which we are faced. Furthermore, as Jean-Paul Sartre used to emphasize, in the end it is we who have to decide and take responsibility for our decisions, even when trying to understand what is the will of God for us, and be responsive to it. This obedience is not something that is inimical to us. Because God is the ground of our being and the goal of our longing, it is in being at one with him that we find peace and fulfilment. In struggling to find the will of God in our lives we are at the same time struggling to find what is deepest and truest within us. D. H. Lawrence began one of his poems with the line. 'All that matters is to be at one with the living God'. This is because God, who is perfect love, desires our wellbeing far more fully and totally than we can possibly imagine for ourselves.

The objection being considered in this chapter that religion fosters immaturity can also arise in people's minds when they think about praying for guidance. To be mature means to stand on one's own feet, to make up one's own mind and to take responsibility for one's own decisions. Is it not infantile to look for the guidance of someone else, even God? This could be seen as an abnegation of our own conscious and responsible free choice. But praying for guidance is not a simple matter of asking and receiving a clear answer. It means thinking as hard as we can about the possibilities open to us and the possible consequences of our actions. It means of course doing this before God, in his presence and with prayer. But the human act of pondering and probing is part of it. Then 'the answer' does not come in the form of ticker-tape across the eyes or voices in the head. What can sometimes happen is that we become clear in our mind, perhaps even with quite a deep conviction, about what is the right course of action for us. That conviction we come to is not something outside of us or alien to us: it is ourselves acting in our most thoughtful and responsible way. For God himself is not outside or alien to us. Through his Holy Spirit he dwells within us and works in and through the mind and heart and conscience which he has given us. Here is a little prayer that brings this out:

> Lord,
> You are the deepest wisdom,
> The deepest truth,
> The deepest love,
> Within me.
> Lead me in your way.

As was stressed in the chapter on hierarchy it was natural in previous generations for people to structure their ethical ideal in terms of command and obedience. Also, there is no doubt that this has often been used to suppress people in the interest of the ruling class. But as was argued there, the concept of hierarchy cannot be totally discarded, even though, on a Christian vision, it is radically transformed. Moreover, the language of command and obedience is so deeply embedded in the scriptures and Christian tradition, it would be difficult to jettison it altogether. However, as has been argued above, this language points to some fundamental truths which, though they may be stated in other ways, need to be safeguarded.

Another salient fact is that the language of command and obedience has become very narrowed in the modern world, to be associated with organizations like the armed services. But in the scriptures the concept is much broader and richer than that. Torah means a whole way of life, one given by God, which leads to our happiness and fulfilment. This is why throughout the Hebrew scriptures the theme 'In thy law is my delight' is such a constant one.

Unfortunately, Christianity is still associated in the public mind with moralizing. It is assumed that the churches' prime function is to teach morality, by which the newspapers usually mean sexual morality, and they then have great fun catching naughty clergy out. But Jesus was the supreme critic of narrow moralizing. Furthermore, time and again he taught that the Torah, God's revealed purpose for humanity, exists for our wellbeing and not the other way round. Most famous of all of course is his saying that 'the Sabbath is made for man and not man for the Sabbath'. While acknowledging the abiding validity of the Torah he kept human need in the forefront of our consideration. When there appeared to be a clash between certain interpretations of the law and human need, he taught that we should keep close to human need.

Christianity first of all offers a vision of what it is to be a human being formed in the divine image. If we are caught up in that vision we see also something of what is required of us. The New Testament is quite clear that the two great injunctions, love of God and love of others, go together. To acknowledge this and to seek to live it out, far from leading to immaturity, is what it is we are made for. We are to grow into nothing less than the full stature of Christ.

CHAPTER 12

Life Today Is Just Too Good for Religion

Organised religion is utterly incompatible with the late twentieth-century post-capitalist consumer world. Christianity is a morality of denial and scarcity, not suitable for our world of superfluity.

(David Starkey)[1]

This critique of religion by David Starkey is fresh and perceptive. No one else, so far as I know, has rejected religion on these grounds. Nevertheless, the phenomenon that he mentions is, from a sociological point of view, undoubtedly a main reason why there has been a falling away from religion by some people.

For the majority of people in the developed world life has improved enormously over the last hundred years. I should however emphasize at the outset that I am dealing with the developed world, not the one billion people living at or below starvation level, to whom I will turn at the end of this chapter. Nor am I at this point writing about the four million people in this country living below widely accepted minimum income levels. To be on the safe side, I am now referring to the two-thirds of the population in the United Kingdom who have never been better off. For us, infant mortality is down, life is healthier and we are all living longer. This is all highlighted by what I call Harries' sod's law.

In order to be happy we need three things – time, money and health. Until recently life has always contrived to deny us one of these. When we are young we have time and our health but no money. When we are middle-aged we have money and our health but no time. When we are old we have time and money but no health. Now, however, there has been a remarkable change. People are retiring early, sometimes in their early fifties, and living longer in a healthy state. There is the third age which might be as long as 30 years, let us say from 55 to 85, before one's powers begin to fail. What is remarkable about the times in which we live is that it is not just the young that are out to enjoy themselves: it is people in the third age, sometimes taking three or more holidays abroad a year.

Driving along, I once saw two camper vans being driven. Each had a placard on the back saying :

> We're too old to work,
> We're too young to die,
> So off we go,
> Just mum and I.

There are other placards you see around expressing the same sentiment, such as 'We are busy spending our children's inheritance'.

The extraordinary contrast this makes with the past can be brought out by one example. In the Fitzwilliam Museum in Cambridge there is a painting by Salvator Rosa (1615–73). It's a fairly gloomy painting and underneath are the words:

> Conception is sinful, birth a punishment, life hard labour,
> death inevitable.

Now, by contrast, for millions of people in the developed world, life is good and feels good. Our world is, as David Starkey said, a 'world of superfluity' and one in which the consumer reigns supreme. From a Christian point of view, much is good about this. Life is meant to be good and feel good. In the Genesis story, after each day of creation God saw what he had made and 'it was good'. The question arises however whether we are grateful for this or whether we take it for granted as something to which we are entitled. The book of Deuteronomy makes the point in words which are still pertinent:

> For the Lord your God is bringing you to a rich land, a land of streams, of springs and underground waters gushing out in hill and valley, a land of wheat and barley, of vines, fig-trees, and pomegranates, a land of olives, oil, and honey. It is a land where you will never live in poverty nor want for anything, a land whose stones are iron-ore and from whose hills you will dig copper. You will have plenty to eat and bless the Lord your God for the rich land that he has given you.
>
> Take care not to forget the Lord your God and do not fail to keep his commandments, laws and statutes which I give you this day. When you have plenty to eat and live in fine houses of your own building, when your herds and flocks increase, and your silver and gold and all your possessions increase too, do not become proud and

forget the Lord your God . . . Nor must you say to yourselves, 'My own strength and energy have gained me this wealth', but remember the Lord your God; it is he that gives you strength to become prosperous. (Deuteronomy 8.7–18)

It is easy today for people to fill their lives with interesting and enjoyable activities. In Nick Hornby's novel *How to be Good* Katie's life gets in such a mess that she is reduced to going to church. She asks the family whether anyone wants to come with her.

David and the children looked at me with some interest, for some time. It's as if, having said something eccentric, I might follow this up by doing something eccentric, like stripping naked or running amok with a kitchen knife. I am suddenly glad that it is not my job to convince people that going to church is a perfectly healthy leisure activity.[2]

There are many healthy leisure activities. And from a religious point of view life and all its blessings remains a gift of God, whether we acknowledge this or not. Sometimes it is only a crisis that brings this home to us and reminds us of the importance of thankfulness for the good things in life. 'We bless thee for our creation, preservation and all the blessings of this life' as the General Thanksgiving in the Book of Common Prayer puts it. William Wordsworth once wrote to a friend:

Theologians may puzzle their heads about dogmas as they will, the religion of gratitude cannot mislead us. Of that we are sure, and gratitude is the handmaid to hope, and hope the harbinger of faith. I look abroad upon nature, I think of the best part of our species, I lean upon my friends and I meditate upon the scriptures, especially the gospel of St John, and my creed rises up of itself, with the ease of an exhalation, yet a fabric of adamant.[3]

David Starkey regards organized religion as utterly incompatible with the late-twentieth-century post-capitalist consumer world, not only because that world is one of superfluity but because 'Christianity is a morality of denial and scarcity'.

The world in which Christianity grew up certainly had its pockets of prosperity, sometimes very large pockets. The ruins of the Hellenistic and Roman cities in the Mediterranean are still enormously impressive. Visitors to Pompeii and Herculaneum will often envy those ancient Romans and their luxurious seaside villas. Nevertheless, even in that well-organized empire, the majority of the population were poor: labourers and slaves, subject to the vagaries of the harvest, oppressive landlords, wars and disease. An interesting debate has taken place in recent years about the social make-up of the early Christian communities. It cannot be assumed, as it once was, that they were all the poorest of the poor. There were some wealthy people among them and the majority were probably what today we would call lower middle class or respectable working class. But the poor certainly were there. In short, the majority, like the vast majority of human beings in every age, have had to struggle to survive. Nor can it be denied that when people struggle to survive they are more likely to be open to any help that religion can give, better able to see themselves as creatures, dependent upon a creator God. Jesus said 'Blessed are you poor.' By this he did not mean simply those who were physically poor. Hence Matthew's version of this 'Blessed are the poor in spirit' safeguards one aspect of the truth. The poor were the *anawim*, the devout poor whose voice we hear time and again in the Psalms. They are people who, losing out in this world, put their trust in God and look to him to vindicate those who do justly but suffer for it.

We have to be careful at this point. Poverty itself is not good. On the contrary, poverty brings ill health and results in a shorter lifespan. It is quite clear from the Hebrew scriptures that God wants life to flourish in all its aspects: the corn and wine and oil to increase, as the Bible puts it. Nevertheless, it is an undoubted fact of experience that people who struggle in life, whether against poverty, illness or other adverse circumstances, are often more open to the spiritual dimension. I will never forget a visit I paid to a community of rural landless poor in Brazil, of whom there are more than four million. In order to stop the flow of these people to the rubbish dumps around Brazil's major cities, the church in Brazil has supported families when they have tried to find land and build a life there. I visited a community of about 30 families living in the most makeshift huts. Yet the spirit of this community was quite extraordinary. They came to meet us across the field, singing joyful songs of praise to God, and presented us with little posies of wild flowers which they had picked along the way. Shortly before we came one of these huts had burnt down, the family losing all its possessions. Other members of the community had rallied round and shared from what little they had. Although this community had now obtained some land and with the help of outside funds was beginning to build more substantial houses and keep some cows, they still saw themselves as very much in solidarity with the whole movement of rural landless poor, sharing their struggle against the organized violence of the big landowners. Interestingly, the leader of this group of families was a young woman in her late twenties. Here was a community determined to fight for basic human rights, living a life of sharing with one another and the wider group, who rooted their life in the grace of God to whom they responded in praise.

Such examples could be multiplied many times over from different parts of the world. Those who visit such communities are conscious of how much we have to receive from them. In the encounter with such people and groups we feel we are coming up against something essential, something which has to all intents and purposes drained away in prosperous communities. They bring home the words of Jesus that in the kingdom of God the first shall be last and the last shall be first. For such communities exhibit the quality and attitudes which find their natural home within God's everlasting kingdom.

So we have a genuine tension here. It is good, God-given and God-willed that many of us no longer live in a world of scarcity. It is also true that Christianity grew up in such a world and has often flourished within it. But this does not make Christianity outdated. On the contrary, it drives us to ask what we might be missing out on and it makes us ask how we can regain such qualities in the very different, more prosperous circumstances of life today.

The other criticism that David Starkey makes is that Christianity is a religion of 'denial' and this makes it out of place in today's prosperous, consumer-driven world. It is certainly true that Jesus called us to deny ourselves, take up our cross and day by day follow him in the way of love. This is as binding on Christians today as it was when first uttered. Furthermore, the world is just as much in need of such unselfishness as it ever was. For despite the prosperity of the developed world, one billion people are living at or below starvation level. In communities where there is this poverty there are high levels of infant mortality, much disease and a much shorter lifespan. In short, there is suffering. Christians, indeed all human beings, are called to stand alongside those who are losing out in this world in their struggle for the basic necessities of life, enough to eat, together with basic healthcare and educational provision. There is in fact enough food to go round in the world as a whole. But because the world economic system is all askew millions starve or live near starvation level while the rest of the world goes in for conspicuous consumption. This is not the place to go into why this crying injustice has come about with, for example, the burden of terrible debt still there for many of the poorest countries in the world. Suffice it to say that many factors have brought it about. Nor should we forget the levels of poverty in the United Kingdom and indeed the United States. There is work to be done here too.

Christianity is indeed a religion of denial, in the sense that we are called to be aware of and respond to the needs of other people: and to allow the claim that those needs make to override our own excessive pursuit of pleasure and luxury. Of course the word 'excessive' implies some standard of what counts as excess, and this will differ from person to person as it differs from culture to culture. But each person is challenged to make a responsible decision in the light of their own circumstances. The point – too obvious to repeat again, but too important not to do so – is that following Jesus by putting into practice his imperative that we love one another is as relevant and binding today as it was in New Testament times.

Starkey's critique of religion is interesting and important. There is no doubt that the developed world in which many of us live is very different and certainly a great deal more prosperous than the world in which the New Testament grew up. But thinking through his criticism brings out more strongly than ever the continuing importance and relevance of Christian belief and practice in the world today.

PART 4

The Case Against Christianity

CHAPTER 13

Christianity Is Anti-Life

Thou hast conquered, O pale Galilean; the world has grown grey
from thy breath.
(Algernon Charles Swinburne, 1837–1909)[1]

This famous phrase sums up for many their dislike of Christianity: it is
anti-life. Jesus is described as pale, and as the poet makes clear in the poem,
that is because of his connection with death and his death-dealing influence. This influence has made the world go grey – not vibrant and
multi-coloured, rich and splendid, but overcast and gloomy.

This feeling about Christianity is widely shared.

Stephen Dedalus, in James Joyce's novel *Portrait of an Artist as a Young
Man*, stands for very many. Stephen was seriously debating in his mind
whether he should become a priest but one day, as he walked on the beach,
life, as he put it, took hold of him. He described his mood in these words:

> His throat ached with a desire to cry aloud, the cry of a hawk or eagle
> on high, to cry piercingly of his deliverance to the winds . . . This was
> the call of life to his soul not the dull gross voice of the world of duties
> and despair, not the inhuman voice that had called him to the pale
> service of the altar. His soul had arisen from the grave of boyhood,
> spurning her grave clothes . . . The clouds were drifting above him
> silently and silently the sea tangle was drifting below him and grey
> warm air was still and a new wild life was singing in his views.

He decides to leave Ireland altogether, and the night before he goes he
wrote in his diary: 'Welcome, O life! I go to encounter for the millionth
time the reality of experience.'[2]

Wilfred Owen too thought of becoming an Anglican priest. In a poem
entitled 'Maundy Thursday', but which should be in fact be called 'Good

Friday' because it describes the service of the Veneration of the Cross which happens on that day, Owen depicts himself coming to kneel and kiss the Cross:

> Then I, too, knelt before that acolyte
> Above the Crucifix I bent my head:
> The Christ was thin, and cold and very dead:
> And yet I bowed, yea, kissed – my lips did cling.
> (I kissed the warm live hand that held the thing).[3]

These passages are so powerful, they need no comment. They should not, however, be interpreted as referring only to sensual experience. What the authors have in mind is as much aesthetic as sensual. When Wilfred Owen was killed there was found among his possessions an envelope on which he had sketched out what he had meant to write to the vicar of the parish where he had served as a lay assistant. Among his criticisms of the religion on offer was that it had no proper place for the aesthetic. Too often Christianity has been not only anti-body and anti-sex, anti this world with all its delights and pleasures, but anti-beauty and anti-art. Few have put it more powerfully than the Welsh priest and poet R. S. Thomas when he wrote:

> Protestantism – the adroit castrator
> Of art; the bitter negation
> Of song and dance and the heart's innocent joy –
> You have botched our flesh and left us only the soul's
> Terrible impotence in a warm world.[4]

All this is a terrible distortion of Christianity. For the Hebrew scriptures are quite clear that creation is good, something to be delighted in. Thank goodness, this has been even more a theme of religious writers and poets down the ages than the negative assessments quoted above.

If creation is fundamentally good, to be enjoyed and delighted in, as the foundation documents of Judaism, Christianity and Islam affirm, what went wrong? There are a number of factors. Manicheism was an influence in the ancient world. Manicheism is quite explicitly dualistic, regarding the material world as in itself evil. The greatest theological influence on Christianity outside the Bible, in both Protestantism and Catholicism, is St Augustine. Augustine went through a Manicheic phase before his conversion to Christianity. But it is doubtful whether he ever fully threw off the influence of that world-denying view. An even more powerful element was the all-pervasive influence of neo-Platonism in the ancient world. Again, neo-Platonism is explicitly dualistic, identifying the spiritual with the soul, which is regarded as trapped in an alien body. Early Christianity was enormously shaped by the wider Platonic environment and took on board many insights from it which were helpful, and it certainly rejected the more extreme forms of neo-Platonism. Yet still some of this dualism crept in. One example of this can be seen in the way the terms *sarx* and *pneuma* have been interpreted for most of Christian history. In the Authorized Version of the Bible *sarx* is translated 'flesh' and *pneuma* is translated 'spirit'. In some of St Paul's letters *sarx* and *pneuma* are strongly contrasted, and is said that there is an unending struggle between them. What St Paul means by *sarx* is the whole of human existence as it is organized against God. But for most of Christian history, *sarx* has simply been understood as the material world with its physical desires. Instead of the proper contrast of the world organized against God and the world shaped by God and at one with him, we have had the contrast of the material and the non-material, the physical and the non-physical.

Then there was the high esteem in which asceticism was held in the ancient world, as it is still in India. The result was that when in the fourth century the more serious-minded Christians wanted to witness to Christ in a society that was becoming lax, when it was becoming fashionable to become a Christian, they thought that one of the best ways in which they could do this was by adopting an ascetic way of life. This was the time when Christians in their thousands went into the deserts of Egypt and Palestine. It was a time when people performed extraordinary feats, like spending the whole of their life on top of a pillar, gathering huge crowds below and performing miracles. This way of witnessing to Christ should not be despised or mocked. But it certainly seems very strange to us. Gladstone was one of our greatest prime ministers, a man of towering intellect and huge achievements. A devout Christian, he regularly flagellated himself as part of his disciplined Christian life. Roy Jenkins has written an excellent biography of Gladstone, a man whom he hugely admires. But you cannot help feeling that there is a great gulf between the urbane, liberal outlook of Jenkins and the late-Victorian mind of Gladstone that could see flagellation as an appropriate aspect of Christian discipleship.

There is one final reason, the most important of all, why Christianity in the past has too often been distorted into a world-denying, anti-life mentality. The fundamental challenge presented to all religions is the clamant, grasping ego; the self which wants to draw attention to itself, impose its will on others and be at the centre of a universe which it controls. The wicked deceit of asceticism, in whatever form, when pursued for its own sake is that it can both cover up or disguise the fundamental problem of egocentricity and at the same time reinforce that egocentricity in its prideful self-assertion. Or, to put it more bluntly, if you have decided to give up all alcohol and rich food and live on one simple meal a day, although this may in many respects be an admirable or even important thing to do, it could hide the fact that it is human pride that is the problem. Furthermore, the ability to live on one simple meal a day might give one a sense of self-satisfaction or superiority. None of this should be taken as an attack on the importance of self-discipline, appropriate abstinence and the desirability of a simple lifestyle. It is simply to point to the perennial temptation to which every religion is prone. There is a further aspect, closely connected with this. Such an understanding of religion can not only reinforce pride, it can blunt one's sensitivity to the needs of other people which are crying out to be met. This is why the Hebrew scriptures are full of prophetic denunciations of distorted religion:

> Since you serve your own interest only on your fast-day
>   and make all your men work the harder,
> since your fasting leads only to wrangling and strife
>   and dealing vicious blows with the fist,
>   on such a day you are keeping no fast
>   that will carry your cry to heaven.
> Is it a fast like this that I require,
>   a day of mortification such as this,
>   that a man should bow his head like a bulrush
>   and make his bed on sackcloth and ashes?
>   Is this what you call a fast,
>   a day acceptable to the Lord?
> Is not this what I require of you as a fast:
>   to loose the fetters of injustice,
>   to untie the knots of the yoke,
>   to snap every yoke
>   and set free those who have been crushed?
> Is it not sharing your food with the hungry,
> taking the homeless poor into your house,
>   clothing the naked when you meet them
> and never evading a duty to your kinsfolk?
>
> (Isaiah 58.3–7)

Jesus stood in this tradition when he criticized certain aspects of the religion of his day. Indeed, he explicitly calls this kind of religion a deathly, death-dealing deadness:

> You are like tombs covered with whitewash; they look well from outside, but inside they are full of dead men's bones and all kinds of filth. So it is with you: outside you look like honest men, but inside you are brim-full of hypocrisy and crime. (Matthew 23.27–28)

Perhaps most famously of all, Paul spells out the truth in his hymn to love, in which he said, using the Authorized Version, 'Though I bestow all my goods to feed the poor, and though I give my body to be burned, and have not charity, it profiteth me nothing' (1 Corinthians 13.3).

Closely connected with this theme is the impression too often made by Christianity that it is negative, concerned to say 'Don't do this' or 'Stop doing that'. And it is certainly true that in the scriptures there are many commandments of a negative kind; and of the Ten Commandments, nine are couched in negative form. All this can give the impression that religion is opposed to what is enjoyable, life-giving and life-enhancing.

The first commandment however is definitely positive in character: we are to love God with all that we are. Furthermore, Jesus summed up all the moral teaching of the Hebrew scriptures in his two great commands, that we are to love God with everything that we have and love our neighbours as ourselves. Nothing could be more positive than that. It is in relation to that overall aim and within that framework that all the other sayings must be seen.

As a young curate I used to go into our local church primary school to teach a few periods of religious education each week – rather unsuccessfully. But one lesson did go really well. I asked the children to imagine that they were on a desert island and that they had to agree a few rules in order to help people live happily together. I suggested that they drew up ten rules. The result was a most remarkable resemblance to the Ten Commandments.

At the very least, then, the Ten Commandments provide a few benchmarks, enabling us to live together without too much squabbling. But perhaps we can go further than that and see them as safety regulations for handling highly dangerous material. The safety regulations connected with a nuclear power plant are absolutely vital; so are the safety regulations connected with a petrol filling station. It is very foolish at the least to start striking matches when filling up the tank with fuel. Our basic human drives can also be highly dangerous. We are not weak, anaemic beings: we are impelled by a number of powerful drives which, if unchecked, can destroy both others and ourselves. It is in this light that we should see the commandments against murdering other people, committing adultery, stealing and lying.

Within the Ten Commandments there are ones which are of a specifically religious, rather than a simply moral character – for example the first commandment that God is the only God, and the second one that we are not to worship idols. Here again, there is something fundamental to human wellbeing. For as human beings we have been created with a capacity to give our all to something, whether it is a football team, our country, political ideology or God. Idolatry, strictly considered, is to treat as ultimate that which is less than ultimate. There may not be very much worshipping of sticks and stones today but there is a great deal of giving of allegiance to things finite rather than the one infinite reality. If there is indeed one true God, the ground of our being and the goal of our longing, then clearly a right relationship with this reality is fundamental to human wellbeing and happiness. If we are giving our total loyalty to something less than this, then everything gets distorted. The seriousness of the choice before us was put in these words by Moses:

> I summon heaven and earth to witness against you this day: I offer you the choice of life or death, blessing or curse. Choose life and then you and your descendants will live; love the Lord your God, obey him and hold fast to him: that is life for you and length of days in the land which the Lord swore to give to your forefathers, Abraham, Isaac and Jacob. (Deuteronomy 30.19–20)

It is life with which Christianity is concerned, true life, authentic life, the life which is wellbeing for others as well as ourselves. The negatives are only there in order to ensure that the raw energy that drives us, what the Book of Common Prayer calls 'Our unruly wills and passions', is channelled in appropriate ways.

Another aspect of the criticism that Christianity is anti-life, is that it is simply boring. Many people, especially children, claim to find church services boring. That is outside the scope of this book. It is the wider accusation that religion itself is boring that is addressed here. If sometimes Christians do convey the impression that religion is boring, something has gone wrong in the way they understand and communicate it. For, to adapt the definition of God given by the great Archbishop of Canterbury Anselm, God must be 'That than which there cannot be a more interesting'. God is by definition the most interesting reality there is. If Christians are conveying something different, then they are not apprehending the true God. The fact is that all of us, Christians and non-Christians alike, tend to stumble through life only half aware. Religion, properly grasped, opens us up to the wondrous reality of things. That is why truly religious people will almost always have an extraordinary zest for life, an interest in things, and will themselves be life-enhancing for others.

In contrast to the distortions that have sometimes crept in to the presentation of Christian truth, Jesus taught that his religion is life-giving. He said, 'I have come that men may have life, and may have it in all its fullness' or, as the Authorized Version puts it, may have life abundantly (John 10.10). In John's gospel, life is the central concept. In the teaching of Jesus as given us in the synoptic gospels, Matthew, Mark and Luke, the leading theme is that of the kingdom of God. Jesus came to proclaim the presence of God's just and gentle rule and invite people to live under it. The phrase 'kingdom of God' does not appear at all in John's gospel; instead, it is replaced by the theme of life.

This life is nothing less than the life of the Godhead, the divine life, focused in the Eternal Son, or Word of God. This life, never absent from creation, but shining in its darkest corners (John 1.4–5) came among us in Jesus. Jesus drew this life from the Father and sought to share it with his friends and followers. This life was released into the world by his death and resurrection. As Christians in every age meditate on the scriptures and receive the body and blood of Christ in the Eucharist, they continue to be fed by the bread of life, a life which unites them to God for ever (John 6). In the passage quoted earlier, Stephen Dedalus says, 'Welcome O life! I go to encounter for the millionth time the reality of experience.' He means something quite specific by the word life, namely 'the reality of experience'. Other people might mean 'living it up' and have in mind a round of parties. People use the same word but mean different things by it. Yet, at the same time, I suspect that there is something behind all these usages that is pointing in the same direction. We all want to wake up in the morning, and when we have banished sleepiness, want the day ahead to be worthwhile and enjoyable. We want to feel that it is good to be alive, that, despite everything, the world is a beautiful and wonderful place; that even in the humdrum tasks of everyday life good things can be achieved. Despite our different shades of meaning, we all want Life with a capital L, rather than mere existence, as T. S. Eliot put it, 'measuring out one's life with coffee spoons'.[5]

From a Christian view this Life is first and foremost a consequence of living at one with the ground of our being. If, moment by moment, we spring forth from the ground of all existence, then the first, indispensable priority must be to be at one with the fount from whom our being flows. Otherwise we simply block or distort or even poison ourselves at the root of our being. Christ came in order that we may, through him, be at one with that fount, be in union with his heavenly Father and ours. Christ comes to take us to himself, and in taking us to himself takes us into the very heart of Godhead.

This life into which Christ takes us, is the life of love, both towards God and other people. The purpose of being on this earth is to grow in that love. No one is totally devoid of the capacity, and within all of us there is the possibility of development. The life of the Godhead which through Christ we have come to share, is nothing less than this life of love. The great theme running through the central chapters of St John's gospel is that those who love Christ are to obey his commands, and his command is that we love one another. If we love one another then God himself will come and dwell within us and that divine presence is nothing less than life (John 13.31, 15—17.26). The same theme runs through the epistles of John:

For God is love; and his love was disclosed to us in this, that he sent his only Son into the world to bring us life. The love I speak of is not our love for God, but the love he showed to us in sending his Son as the remedy for the defilement of our sins. If God thus loved us, dear friends, we in turn are bound to love one another. Though God has never been seen by any man, God himself dwells in us if we love one another; his love is brought to perfection within us. (1 John 4.9–12)

This life is life here and now lived with a particular spirit and quality. But because it is a life of union with God and the developing life of God within us, it is a life that nothing can destroy. This is the theme of the haunting story of the raising of Lazarus. The raising of Lazarus was a sign that even now, through Jesus, we can receive a life that lives in God for ever. Martha says to Jesus that she knows her brother will rise again on the last day. To this Jesus responds, 'I am the resurrection and the life; he that believeth in me, though he were dead, yet shall he live: And whosoever liveth and believeth in me shall never die' (John 11.25–26). It is for this reason that the Life which Jesus brings is sometimes termed 'eternal life' or 'everlasting life'. Because it is a life which opens up to God now, it is one which opens up to him for all eternity.

One crucial feature of this life is that it is all-inclusive. One of the problems of modern hedonism, the pursuit of pleasure for its own sake, the philosophy that seems to run through so many of our colour supplements and glossy magazines, is that it may be all right for those who are in a position to pursue pleasure but no good for anyone else and no good for any of us in the end when we are struck down by strokes or are wasting away with cancer. If life has an ultimate meaning and purpose it cannot simply be in terms of pleasure. There are so many millions of people in the world for whom the pleasures of life are pretty minimal – children born with crippling disease, those who have accidents, those whose circumstances severely constrict what they can do or achieve, those whose temperaments, through no fault of their own, make satisfying long-term relationships very hard to achieve, and so on. Then in the end we are all 'Sans teeth, sans eyes, sans taste, sans everything.'[6] A Christian understanding offers a way of life which includes everyone and every stage of our human existence, including the last. For life is not calculated simply in terms of pleasure and pain, however important these are to us at any one moment. There is a much larger, wider calculus of growth in the love of God and growth in the love of other people. It is in this scale that in the end all things will be measured.

Those who understand the nature of this life and truly live it have a capacity to enjoy the world and its blessings which cannot be rivalled.

Undoubtedly there have been expressions of Christianity which have been gloomy and life denying. But in every age there have been Christians who have savoured life with an intensity sharpened by their faith – from St Paul's sense of 'having nothing yet possessing all things', through St Augustine's deeply moving passages about the beauty of the world, and people as diverse as Thomas Traherne and Gerard Manley Hopkins right to the present day. For millions of people the words of G. K. Chesterton would apply:

> I do not think there is anyone who takes quite such a pleasure in things being themselves as I do. The startling wetness of water excites and intoxicates me: the fieriness of fire, the steeliness of steel, the unutterable muddiness of mud.

CHAPTER 14

Christianity Bangs On About Guilt and Sin

Every Sunday we had to kneel together and say with the priest:

> Almighty and most merciful Father; We have erred, and strayed
> from thy ways like lost sheep. We have followed too much the
> devices and desires of our own hearts. We have offended against
> thy holy laws. We have left undone those things which we ought to
> have done; And we have done those things which we ought not to
> have done. And there is no health in us. But Thou, O Lord, have
> mercy upon us, miserable offenders.

> Even as a schoolboy I found this demeaning and untrue. I had no idea
> what holy law I was supposed to have offended against and I objected
> strongly to being likened to a lost sheep and having to declare
> publicly that I had been a miserable offender.
>
> (Ludovic Kennedy)[1]

Even when we have made allowances for the strong sixteenth-century
prose, too strong for many people's tastes, Ludovic Kennedy is making a
serious point. His feelings when faced with the Church's language about
sin and guilt would be widely shared today. In fact Kennedy is making four
points, not one, all of which interrelate and reinforce one another.

1 'I had no idea what holy law I was supposed to have offended against.'
2 The description of himself as 'a lost sheep' and 'a miserable offender'
  seem simply untrue. He did not feel like that.
3 Having to say these things about himself struck him as 'demeaning'.
4 The Church is criticized for trying to inculcate and reinforce such
  attitudes.

Although Kennedy's example is taken from the Book of Common Prayer, the liturgies of the Church today and the attitude of many Christians would still incur Kennedy's critique. The chaplain of a college at Cambridge once asked a Christian undergraduate how he saw his role as a student. He replied, in an accent shaped by Scottish Protestantism, 'To convince men of their vileness in the eyes of God.' This was before the days when women were admitted to men's colleges, though no doubt he meant women as well.

The fact that Ludovic Kennedy felt as he did when he knelt in chapel at Eton and the fact that his response resonates widely, indicates the profound cultural change that has taken place over the last hundred years. The American theologian Paul Tillich believed that each age had its own besetting anxiety. At the time when the New Testament was written this was a sense that the world was in the grip of an impersonal fate. During the late medieval and Reformation period people were gnawed by a sense of guilt, and in our time it is predominantly a feeling of meaninglessness which oppresses us. What this historical analysis brings out is that whereas in the late medieval and Reformation period the Christian faith could be powerfully preached as a deliverance from sin and a sense of guilt, it is much more difficult to do that today when there has been a widespread loss of a sense of sin and, if people feel guilty, those feelings are buried pretty deep.

Rose Macaulay, in wonderful, breathless historical sweep wrote:

And, while I am on sin, I have often thought that it is a most strange thing that this important part of human life, the struggle that almost every one has about good and evil, cannot now be talked of without embarrassment, unless of course one is in church.

Once people used to talk about being good and being bad, they wrote about it in letters to their friends, and conversed about it freely; the Greeks did this, and the Romans, and then, after life took a Christian turn, people did it more than ever, and all through the Middle Ages they did it, and through the Renaissance, and drama was full of it, and heaven and hell seemed for ever round the corner, with people struggling on the borderlines and never knowing which way it was going to turn out, and in which of these two states they would be spending their immortality, and this led to a lot of conversation about it all, and it was extremely interesting and exciting. And they went on talking about their conflicts all through the seventeenth and eighteenth and nineteenth centuries, and James Boswell, who of course was even more interested in his own character and behaviour than most people are, wrote to this friends, 'My great object is to attain a proper conduct in life. How sad will it be if I turn out no better than I am' . . . they went on like this through most of the nineteenth century, even when they were not evangelicals or tractarians or anything like that, and nineteenth-century novels are full of such interesting conversations, and the Victorian agnostics wrote to one another about it continually, it was one of their favourite topics, for the weaker they got on religion the stronger they got on morals, which used to be the case more then than now.

I am not sure when all this died out, but it has now become very dead.[2]

The reasons for this major cultural shift are many. There will no doubt be underlying economic and political reasons as well as social ones. But some of the indicators of this profound change are, first, our inclination to be less judgemental, at least about some wrongdoing. Even when Ludovic Kennedy was at Eton more liberal attitudes, for example towards punishment, were beginning to gain ground. Second, there is so much less certainty about the objectivity of moral judgements. All that comes under the heading of postmodernism indicates our lack of confidence, compared with previous generations, about what is right and what is wrong. Third, the reality of God is not in the forefront of our culture, so that even if people do sometimes feel that they have wronged a fellow human being, they find it difficult to feel that they have wronged, or sinned against God. Fourth, this is linked in particular with changes in sexual morality. For much of European history the Church tried to keep a tight control over people's sexual mores. Not only did they teach these in schools and churches, until the Reformation they could control people's sexual lives through the confessional and after the Reformation could ensure that naming and shaming was part of the culture when it came to sexual sins. All this changed, as Philip Larkin put in, in 1963. The widespread availability of contraception and the general loosening of traditional restraints resulted in what was called permissiveness.

I am not arguing that everything has 'gone to the dogs'. Nor is it necessarily true that our time is more morally lax than previous generations. In many respects we are clearly more morally aware, for example on issues like child abuse, racism and equal opportunities. But for the four reasons suggested, and no doubt others, the kind of assumptions on the basis of which the Gospel was preached a hundred years ago no longer pertain. There is a widespread, almost universal, loss of any sense of sin.

At the same time, there is an extraordinary paradox. For the world in which we live is one in which the most terrible things happen. This century has seen the Shoah, as a result of which more than six million Jews were deliberately exterminated just because they were Jews. More than 28 million people were killed in Stalin's purges in the Soviet Union. Recent years have seen the most brutal face-to-face hackings to death in Rwanda.

And if we thought we could distance ourselves from what was happening in Africa, a no less cruel slaughter has taken place in Bosnia and Kosovo. Furthermore, almost every novel, the majority of films and many TV programmes depict a world of violence. We live in a world where wicked things happen on a massive scale as well as day by day in the domestic situations which we read about in our newspapers.

There is a further paradox. We live in a highly individualistic age. The bonds of community are perhaps weaker than they have ever been, and people feel themselves to be isolated individuals. At the same time there is little sense of personal responsibility for the ills of the world. One example of this, now often remarked on in the newspapers, is the way that no one is prepared to take responsibility in public affairs when something goes badly wrong. When there is a disaster or a scandal it is rare now for anyone to be brought to account; heads, far from rolling, retire gracefully on a good pension. Day by day the human suffering brought about by human wickedness comes before us on our television screens. Yet we have very little sense of personal responsibility for our share in the wickedness of the world.

One reason for this paradoxical state of affairs is in itself good and very much to be welcomed. We emphasize the importance of people valuing themselves, of self-worth, self-esteem. This has sometimes taken a valuable political form, as it did with the rise of the black consciousness movement and a feeling among people who have been oppressed for so many centuries that 'black is beautiful'. It is very much present now in women's movements, as women, who have in many respects been oppressed for so long, and often still are, struggle to build up their sense of self-esteem. It is now widely recognized that children need a sense of their own worth and value and that they are much more likely to learn well and behave in a responsible manner if they have this sense than if they are beset by feelings of worthlessness, inadequacy and failure. This may have its dangers, of moral complacency for example, or of a failure to recognize wrong to be wrong. But the trend today to help people think well of themselves, rather than badly – to build people up rather than make them feel small – is a vital moral insight that we should not lose. From a Christian point of view, it conforms to a fundamental tenet of the Gospel.

Any approach to the questions of wrongdoing today must begin by taking seriously what Ludovic Kennedy has written and the feelings of those millions who recognize in his words their own experience. This means a recognition that a major cultural shift has taken place. No doubt some will say that although people today don't feel guilty, they ought to feel guilty and it is the job of the Church to stir up feelings of guilt within them as a prelude to offering the Gospel as a liberation from such guilt. Apart from anything else the trouble with this strategy is that the wrong people tend to feel guilty. There are some people who are beset by feelings of guilt. This has little to do with objective wrongdoing and, according to Melanie Klein, has a great deal to do with early breastfeeding difficulties. Such people need to be liberated from these irrational feelings. Unfortunately, any attempt by the Church or anyone else to inculcate a deeper sense of sin will only stir up and reinforce the feelings of guilt from which such people need to be delivered. At the same time, the complacent, the smug, the self-righteous, the morally obtuse and prideful will find yet another stratagem to ward off any inclination to feel such guilt themselves.

One difficulty connected with this theme is the alleged moral relativism of our time, all that is associated with the phrase postmodernism. Behind this lie a number of factors. There is the historical sense with which we are all now imbued, the sense that society has evolved and every age has its own particular perspectives and moral emphasis. This is closely connected with all the work done by anthropologists and sociologists in recent decades in relation to different cultures and their varying outlooks. There is also the work of philosophers and their very divided views about the nature of moral statements, let alone their contents. This is not the place to go into this complex subject, though there are some signs now that post-modernism itself is passing and we are moving into a new era of post postmodernism.

Three simple points might be made, all of which of course are worthy of a great deal of amplification. First, whatever differences of emphasis there may be with other periods in history or other cultures, and indeed whatever differences there may be in what is regarded as right and wrong, there are a fair number of fundamental moral insights on which all human beings, except psychopaths, would agree – for example, that torturing people is wrong. This is not unrelated to the second point, namely the great body of international human rights law which has emerged since the Second World War. Future historians may very well look back on this as one of the great achievements of the post-war era. This sets out in legal form a great deal of what in the past would have gone under the heading of Natural Law, those fundamental moral judgements capable of being discerned by every human being in every culture. There is then the third, more philosophical point, that it is possible for people from very different cultures to communicate. For example, we could take the extreme of a Buddhist from a Buddhist culture talking to a Muslim from an Islamic culture. The two religions are very different in outlook, as are the cultures that they have shaped. But it remains possible for that Buddhist and that Muslim to communicate with each other about their moral values. The very possibility of communicating, of comparing one thing with another, implies a realm of discourse and a dimension of value that is shared.

Not unrelated to this is the fact that the Church itself so often seems divided on moral issues. If the Church is calling people to recognize objective standards of right and wrong but itself is uncertain about what these are, this is less than convincing for the outside world. But again, the extent of the division can be greatly exaggerated. What unites the churches is far more than what divides them. For example, though it is true that the Roman Catholic Church teaches that abortion is wrong under all circumstances, the Church of England, although it allows some exceptions, regards those exceptions as very few indeed. The whole thrust of its teaching is fundamentally in sympathy with that of the Roman Catholic Church. We do however have to face the fact that genuinely new issues arise and there is bound to be a period of turbulence and disagreement until the Church comes to a settled mind on an issue. This has been true in relation to many medical advances as it applies in relation to same-sex relationships. There are genuine issues here and it is not surprising that the Church should take some time in thinking through the implications of new discoveries or new ways of looking at traditional Christian teaching. Sometimes it does indeed seem that all is disagreement and confusion. But in fact there is usually to be found a profound level of agreement on fundamentals, and where there is disagreement, there is the Christian conviction that each one of us has some capacity to discern what is the right course of action in our own circumstances and we should respect the conscientious decisions of those with whom we disagree.

For a Christian, the place to begin and end is with the unique value of each human person. As Desmond Tutu likes to say, 'God loves each one of us as though we were the only person in the world.' It is because God loves us that we exist in the first place. It is because God loves us that he sent his Son Jesus Christ to draw us into his presence and live with his life. The parables that Jesus told, of the farmer who scoured the countryside for the one lost sheep, the housewife who clambered all over the floor looking for the lost coin and the father who scanned the horizon for the homecoming of his son, teach the extent to which God goes for our sake. Jesus, through his example of going out of his way to eat with those whom society marginalized and rejected, ending up crucified between two thieves on the cross, lived out that love for us. If God so loves us, how can we not value ourselves?

At the same time, it is part of God's love for us that he has such a glorious vocation and destiny in mind for us. As the early Fathers of the Church liked to say, we are made in God's image but we are called to grow into his likeness. This call came first to the people of Israel. 'You shall be holy, because I, the Lord your God, am holy' (Leviticus 19.2). Jesus put it before us in uncompromising terms: 'You, therefore, must be perfect, as your heavenly father is perfect' (Matthew 5.48) or, as a modern version puts it, 'There must be no limit to your goodness, as your heavenly Father's goodness knows no bounds' (The Revised English Bible). If God had loved us less he would be less ambitious for us. It is because he loves us so much that he wants us to share his life to the full, to become more and more like him in his total self-giving.

This means that the more a person has come to know God, the closer they have come to him, the more aware they have become of their own bundle of feelings (not all of them savoury), and of their own mixed motives.

Over the portal of the temple of Apollo at Delphi in ancient Greece was the saying 'Know thyself'. Knowing ourselves is not easy: it can be painful. This is the theme of a poem by Thomas Hardy:

> A cry from the green-grained sticks of the fire
> Made me gaze where it seemed to be:
> 'Twas my own voice talking therefrom to me
> On how I had walked when my sun was higher –
> My heart in its arrogancy.
>
> *'You held not to whatsoever was true'*
> Said my own voice talking to me:
> *'Whatsoever was just you were slack to see;*
> *Kept not things lovely and pure in view,'*
> Said my own voice talking to me.
> *'You slighted her that endureth all,'*
> Said my own voice talking to me;
> *'Vaunteth not, trusteth hopefully;*
> *That suffereth long and is kind withal,'*
> Said my own voice talking to me.
>
> *'You taught not that which you set about,'*
> Said my own voice talking to me;
> *'That the greatest of things is Charity . . .'*
> – And the sticks burnt low, and the fire went out,
> And my voice ceased talking to me.[3]

It is also a theme of a number of T. S. Eliot's plays, as well as 'The Four Quartets', where he wrote:

> And last, the rending pain of re-enactment
> Of all that you have done, and been; the shame
> Of motives late revealed, and the awareness
> Of things ill done and done to others' harm
> Which once you took for exercise of virtue.

Then fools' approval stings, and honour stains.
From wrong to wrong the exasperated spirit
Proceeds, unless restored by that refining fire
Where you must move in measure, like a dancer.[4]

The other point that it is important to note, is that we are all bound up with one another. This is not to take away from a sense of personal responsibility. Nor is it fruitful to try to make people feel guilty for what happened years before they were born or what is totally outside their control. But through his incarnation Christ is united to the whole of humanity, and to be in Christ is to stand before our heavenly father, not as an isolated individual but with the humanity for which Christ lived and died and rose again. When in the liturgy the Church comes before God it prays, 'O Lamb of God, who takes away the sin of the world'. It is the sin of the world – the sin of Rwanda, the sin of Bosnia and Kosovo, the sin of a world in which the poorest countries are burdened by debt and a billion people live at or below starvation level because the whole world economic system is flawed and skewed as a result of multiple injustices that have got into it – that we bring before God.

The purpose of thinking like this, in solidarity with all humanity, is to bring about change, both in ourselves and in the world as a whole. It is not to berate oneself or to make oneself feel mean and small and dirty. But constructive change can begin with a gentle self-awareness. For example, when an institution, whether it is the Church, the police or the law, goes in for gender awareness training or racism awareness training this is because of a recognition that not necessarily deliberately but perhaps quite inadvertently, the whole institution and therefore the majority of members within it, have taken on certain cultural assumptions and presuppositions that we now recognize it is important to grow out of. When the 'Drop the Debt' campaign brings home to the world the massive suffering inflicted by the burden of debt in the poorest countries, this is not to make those of us in the developed world beat our breasts: it is to make us aware that something has gone radically wrong and that action can and must be taken to right a fundamental injustice. In this work we will all have a share. But first we must see that there is actually a wrong that needs to be righted and that we all have a responsibility to do what we can.

Guilt itself is not a healthy motivator of action. That is why Jewish people are less and less happy about wanting a new, more constructive relationship with the Christian world on the basis of guilt for the Shoah. They want this new relationship to be built on a recognition of the validity and vitality of modern Judaism. In a similar way, whether it is to do with ending racism, the subjugation of women, or world debt, it is the objective reality of the situation facing us that is important, and our sense of responsibility to address it. Facing the facts and responding with appropriate thought and action is what following Jesus requires. As to our motives, they are of course all mixed. But as T. S. Eliot put it, 'The purification of the motive' is 'in the ground of our beseeching.'[5]

CHAPTER 15

Christians Eat God

Nor was the ceremony of the Eucharist exclusively Christian. It stems from the ancient right of sacrificial cannibalism and the eating of totem animals; for example Red Indian tribes who held the buffalo to be sacred used to kill and eat one once a year in order to absorb its strength. Among the Aztecs a huge image of the corn god Huitzilopochtli was set up, made of dough and the blood of infants which by a process of trans-substantiation become the god himself and was eaten . . . In a similar way the early Christians celebrated the last supper not to obtain remission for the forgiveness of sins, but to gain eternal life.

(Ludovic Kennedy)[1]

People who are groping their way into Christianity can suddenly find themselves shocked and horrified, though they may be too polite to express such feelings, at the sacrificial, cannibalistic language of the Eucharist. This is true whether we are talking about a Roman Catholic Mass or a Protestant Lord's Supper. The meaning in different traditions may vary but the language is the same, stemming as it does from the New Testament. My concern here is not with the meaning of the rite, except to remark that there has been an extraordinary degree of convergence about this between churches which were bitterly divided at the Reformation. My concern is with the language and the stark effect this can have on a modern sensibility. Nor does this just affect outsiders or those who are feeling their way towards belief. A good number of lifetime churchgoers feel inwardly uneasy about what the language is suggesting. For example, the much loved Prayer of Humble Access in the Book of Common Prayer says:

Grant us therefore, gracious Lord, so to eat the flesh of thy dear son Jesus Christ, and to drink his blood, that our sinful bodies may be made clean by his body, and our souls washed through his most precious blood, and that we may evermore dwell in him, and he in us.

Common Worship continues this wording.

As Kennedy rightly points out, all this suggests that in the Eucharist Christians are eating God and what they are doing has some continuity with sacrificial rites of earlier people in many different cultures. Such an idea can seem, literally, revolting to many people today, and this reaction has to be honestly faced.

The place to start in trying to understand better what is happening and see this in a totally different light, is not with the eucharistic rite itself but in considering what it is to be created at all. Jews, Christians and Muslims believe that everything that exists does so only because God wills it to exist. All that is in being comes into being from him. Moment by moment and every moment of the long evolutionary process, the universe wells up from the fount of all existence. This applies not only to our physical existence but to our spiritual life and moral qualities as well. Christians – and others – emphasize that all that comes to us in the way of moral improvement and spiritual growth comes from the grace of God. All is given by him. Of course, from another point of view, the choices we make are ours and the struggle is ours. There is a paradox here. As St Paul put it: 'By God's grace I am what I am, nor has his grace been given to me in vain; on the contrary, in my labours I have outdone them all – not I, indeed, but the grace of God working with me' (1 Corinthians 15.10). This means that God not only gives us our physical existence, he gives us our spiritual life and moral qualities; in short, he gives us himself, insofar as we are growing in love. For insofar as we are growing in love we are allowing the life of God, who is love, to dwell in us and work through us. This is to put it in terms of the individual. But although in Christianity each individual is summoned to responsibility, in the end our vision of life is not individualistic. The end to which all points is the communion of saints, a communion of people bound and bonded together by love, whose individuality shines more brightly, and only shines, because each is given wholly to others.

In the Bible this communion of love is symbolized as a great feast, and this is a key image in the teaching of Jesus. Many of his parables use the picture of a wedding feast or banquet. At one point he said, 'Many, I tell you, will come from east and west to feast with Abraham, Isaac, and Jacob in the kingdom of Heaven' (Matthew 8.11). One version of the Last Supper narrative points to this:

Then he took a cup, and after giving thanks he said, 'Take this and share it among yourselves; for I tell you, from this moment I shall drink from the fruit of the vine no more until the time when the kingdom of God comes.' (Luke 22.17–18)

This is why the Eucharist, among other things, has always been seen as an anticipation of the heavenly banquet, a foretaste and pledge of the time when all God's people will sit at his table.

Eating together is a basic and essential expression of human solidarity. One of the saddest features of modern life is the high percentage of families who rarely, if ever, sit down for a meal together. One indication of this is that the traditional Oxo advertisement of a family sitting around a table together has now been withdrawn because it no longer corresponds to the reality of modern life. Nevertheless, what we do with our friends is invite them to a meal. One of the distinctive features of the ministry of Jesus was that he went out of his way to eat with, to have table fellowship with, those whom society as a whole rejected and despised. Psychologists know that this eating together has powerful effects upon us, for good and ill. A child at a table ingests not only food but the atmosphere. They take into themselves the love and fun and laughter – or the acrimony and hostility. It is not surprising that today much illness takes the form of eating disorders. People sometimes dismiss symbols as mere symbols. But there are certain symbols that have a sacramental quality, when the symbol and that which is symbolized are a unity and the symbol profoundly affects our wellbeing, emotional and spiritual. Quakers rightly emphasize that every meal is a sacrament of that kind, every meal a Eucharist.

Moment by moment God invites us to feast at the table of life. He beckons us to our seat around the table of loving community. His love goes on pressing us as in George Herbert's famous poem:

> Love bade me welcome: yet my soul drew back,
>   Guiltie of dust and sinne.
> But quick-ey'd Love, observing me grow slack
>   From my first entrance in,
> Drew nearer to me, sweetly questioning,
>   If I lack'd any thing.
> A guest, I answer'd, worthy to be here:
>   Love said, You shall be he.
> I the unkinde, ungratefull? Ah my deare,
>   I cannot look on thee.
> Love took my hand, and smiling did reply,
>   Who made the eyes but I?
> Truth Lord, but I have marr'd them: let my shame

Go where it doth deserve.
And know you not, sayes Love, who bore the blame?
My deare, then I will serve.
You must sit down, sayes Love, and taste my meat:
So I did sit and eat.[2]

In the Eucharist two images come together: that of the great feast of life, the heavenly banquet to which Jesus invites us, and that of feeding on the life of God himself. As pointed out earlier, all that is comes from God and he wills to give us not only physical life but spiritual life, and that spiritual life is nothing less than his presence and his love filling us. We need to take that more deeply into ourselves even than the food we digest. This idea of feeding on God himself is not just an abstract idea. In Christ he has come among us in order to give his life for us. Through the cross, his body broken and his blood shed, his life goes out into the world and becomes the food for every eucharistic table. That is why there is an integral relationship between sacrifice and feeding on God. In Christianity it is the life of Christ given for us and for our salvation that gives us eternal life. This is the theme of the sixth chapter of St John's gospel in which Jesus meditates on the theme 'I am the bread of life'. The imagery is startling and uncompromising:

> This led to a fierce dispute among the Jews. 'How can this man give us his flesh to eat?' they said. Jesus replied, 'In truth, in very truth I tell you, unless you eat the flesh of the Son of Man and drink his blood you can have no life in you. Whoever eats my flesh and drinks my blood possesses eternal life and I will raise him up on the last day. My flesh is real food; my blood is real drink. Whoever eats my flesh and drinks my blood dwells continually in me and I dwell in him. As the living Father sent me, and I live because of the Father, so he who eats me shall live because of me. This is the bread which came down from heaven; and it is not like the bread which our fathers ate: they are dead, but whoever eats this bread shall live for ever.' (John 6.52–58)

It should be noted that the theme of this chapter of John is not only about or mainly about the Eucharist: it is about Christ himself whom we receive into ourselves through his teaching and obedience to his word in the scriptures as well as in the Holy Communion.

The imagery of the Eucharist can indeed be startling and shocking for people. It brings to mind what we tend to regard as the primitive customs of primitive people which we have now outgrown. But those earlier rites of earlier people were a groping after the truth, in however distorted form that truth was manifested. The truth is that all that exists comes from God and that he wills to dwell within us with his life of love. In order that this might come about he himself came among us and gave his life for us. He is the bread of life who feeds us on himself. He gives us the food of immortality as we sit with others at God's table in the feast of life.

CHAPTER 16

Christianity Is Just for Wimps

> Come down and speak to the men of ability
> On the Sevenoaks platform and tell them
> That at your St Nicholas the faith
> Is not exclusive in the fools it chooses
> That the vain, the ambitious and the highly sexed
> Are the natural prey of the incarnate Christ.
>
> (C. H. Sisson)[1]

C. H. Sisson's favoured form of Anglicanism is that of the late seventeenth century. In recent years he has therefore become somewhat disillusioned with the Church of England. Nevertheless religious themes recur in his poetry, as in his poem 'A Letter to John Donne' from which the above verse is taken. Sisson begins by saying that he understands John Donne well enough:

> First, that you were a man of ability
> Eaten by lust and by the love of God.

He contrasts this with the men of ability he sees standing on Sevenoaks platform every day 'Whom ambition drives as they drive the machine' but whose ambition seems confined to operating computers successfully. In the face of that, he says to John Donne, 'Bring out your genitals and your theology.'

Sisson is dismissive of these commuters but what makes him really angry is the clergyman climbing into the pulpit where John Donne once preached, a sexless creature and a fool. What makes John Donne different from such clergy and those people on Sevenoaks platform is his dual obsession: love – not lust – for women and love of God. For:

> The love of God comes readily
> To those who have most need.

A feeling people often have about religion but are usually too polite to express, is that it is for failures. The assumption is that if we are successful in our personal and professional lives then we have no need of this crutch. Religion, in short, is for wimps, those who can't really make a go of life. There is an important truth hidden here. People are indeed more receptive to God when something has gone wrong in their lives. This will be borne out by every parish priest. It is when someone is bereaved that, perhaps for the first time for many years, they discover the need for prayer and church. They find in religion a genuine consolation, particularly if they have been sensitively ministered to by a good parish priest, which they very often are. Again, every parish priest knows that in the congregation will be a number of people who have been divorced and perhaps remarried. A crisis or breakdown in a close relationship can make a person feel very vulnerable and in need of help. This opens them up to the possibility of help from God. Or it may have been a difficulty from much earlier back. Perhaps the person lost one or both parents as a child or experienced illness as a young person. This made them vulnerable at an early age and through this they found real strength to cope.

It is possible to disparage the experience of such people: to be understanding but in the end dismissive on the grounds that if everything was going well for them they would have no need. The matter can, however, be looked at very differently. As Monica Furlong put it, 'After experiencing great pain or isolation we often have the feeling that we have seen through the superficiality of our lives and perceived a great truth about the way things are.'

When we go through a bad patch, for whatever reason, we are conscious of coming up against the grain of the universe: the important, deep truth about the way things are. As Monica Furlong said, we can realize how petty and superficial our lives have been up to that point.

The great psychologist Jung said that most of his patients were middle-aged and that in most of them there was at bottom a spiritual crisis. A person had perhaps been living dynamically but outwardly for the 20 years before, building a career or a family. Then, in middle age, the neglected inner, spiritual side pushes through, causing a breakdown.

There is another truth, a hard one, in the criticism that religion is only for wimps. It is that for most of the time we are driven by vanity, greed, lust and ambition of various kinds. This itself clouds our vision of God. Moreover, in such a state of mind, we inevitably marginalize religion both in ourselves and in other people. It does not serve our purpose. We cannot use it to further our vanity, greed, lust or ambition – or not usually anyway. Then, if we get what we want, we usually think that it is entirely by our own efforts. We are self-satisfied and desire to be beholden to no one. Jesus once said to a man of the ruling class, 'How hard it is for the wealthy to enter the kingdom of God! It is easier for a camel to go through the eye of an needle than for a rich man to enter the kingdom of God' (Luke 18.24).

Being rich or a member of the ruling class is not the only way of being successful; there are many other ways to which the words of Jesus are equally applicable.

The first, fierce rejection of Christianity on the grounds that it was only for the weak was made by the German philosopher Nietzsche. He argued that Christianity is for slaves and the downtrodden, not for the strong. Indeed, it encourages and celebrates weakness and so perpetuates (and inculcates into the divine) those resentments born of oppression. No doubt Nietzsche's aim was a laudable one, to get people to stand on their own feet and take responsibility for their lives, not being imprisoned by their circumstances but courageous in wanting to shape a new future. Unfortunately his philosophy was appropriated by the Nazis and the extreme right wing. And it is easy to see how his concept of a superman creating a bold new future could lend itself to cruel arrogance. Those who are not supermen are to be despised and the more extreme forms of weakness eliminated. Christianity too, particularly in the form of liberation theology, wants people to stand up and challenge their oppressive surroundings. But it is a distinctive characteristic of liberation theology that it is above all the poor who are God's instrument in doing this. For they are the ones who are most open to being used as such instruments and who are most likely to hold on to the fundamental insight that we belong together, in solidarity with one another, as frail human beings and recipients of God's grace. A Nietzschean philosophy, despising the appeal of Christianity to the weak, can very quickly set itself above those moral norms which are recognized by all moderately decent people.

Christianity is not a cult of failure. We believe passionately that in the end God's purpose of love will prevail. Furthermore, even a cursory reading of history reveals some extraordinary strong, powerful people, women and men, for whom Christian belief has been at the centre of their life. In the modern world, we need to think only of the Roman Catholic priests and bishops in Latin America, like Helder Camara, who has stood up to oppression; countless Christians, black and white, who often at great cost opposed apartheid; those Christians, who again so often at the cost of their life, kept the faith alive under Communist rule in the former Soviet Union. These were people of extraordinary spiritual strength who inspired and encouraged others in their own time and continue to be an inspiration to future generations. By any definition of the word, these are strong people. Yet all of them would have acknowledged that a sense of our weakness, emptiness and dependence upon the ground of all being, together with a profound sense of gratitude to the grace of God in Jesus Christ, was at the centre of their life.

When St Paul wrote to Christians in Corinth he said:

My brothers, think what sort of people you are, whom God has called. Few of you are men of wisdom, by any human standard; few are powerful or highly born. Yet, to shame the wise, God has chosen what the world counts folly, and to shame what is strong, God has chosen what the world counts weakness. He has chosen things low and contemptible, mere nothings, to overthrow the existing order. (1 Corinthians 1.26–28)

The principle which Paul saw at work in the congregation to whom he ministered he also saw at work in himself. He said:

As for me, brothers, when I came to you, I declared the attested truth of God without display of fine words or wisdom. I resolved that while I was with you I would think of nothing but Jesus Christ – Christ nailed to the cross. I came before you weak, nervous, and shaking with fear. (1 Corinthians 2.1–2)

Later he wrote to the Corinthians about a strange illness which afflicted him. No one quite knows what this was but Paul wrote, 'Three times I begged the Lord to rid me of it, but his answer was: "My grace is all you need; power comes to its full strength in weakness".' It is when we are most conscious of our weakness, our inadequacy, our emptiness or our failure that we are most open to be filled by the presence and power of God. This is because there is a radical dependence of all things upon the ground of our being. Moment by moment everything that exists flows from him. Therefore when we consciously realize that radical dependence, when we turn away from our own pride and self-sufficiency to draw from that deep well, we find a living spring filling up within us.

This is not to advocate a cult of failure. On the contrary, as has been emphasized elsewhere in this book, God wants the world to flourish in every aspect. And when people flourish, whether or not they acknowledge the giver of the good gifts they enjoy, the only appropriate response is one of thanks to that giver. When I was a parish priest I once a visited a council flat – nothing grand – but everything in it attractive and comfortable. The couple had decorated it themselves with bright modern wallpapers. He was a skilled tradesman doing a job he enjoyed and this brought in a steady income. As we sat and talked his wife did the ironing – an attractive girl – and between them both was an obvious warmth and affection. They had married young and worked through their early difficulties, which they admitted to me with a disarming openness. Their two children came in, sheer delight to behold. There were warm goodnight kisses all round before the children went off to bed. A family with everything going for them. Silently I wanted to say 'Laus Deo'. The couple also happened to say, just by the way, 'I'm afraid we are not at all religious.'

There are many reasons why people are or are not religious. In the end only God knows. But whether that family were religious or not, for me, as a person of faith, there was so much there for which to give thanks. The Welsh poet R. S. Thomas has a poem called 'The Priest' whose last verse reads:

> 'Crippled soul,' do you say?
> Looking at him
> From the minds height; 'limping through life
> On his prayers. There are other people
> In the world, sitting at table,
> Contented, though the broken body
> And shed blood are not on the menu.'
>
> 'Let it be so,' I say. 'Amen amen.'[2]

I like this poem because it reflects the strength of the non-believer, insofar as it is that, and leaves the believer to go on his own way firm in his own conviction, despite the dismissive thought that he is 'limping through life on his prayers'.

Thank God there are many good, decent people in the world, like that young family I visited, even though religion is not a natural part of their life. Yet, if we are honest, most of us have a range of motives, not all of them noble. In a brilliant metaphor Malcolm Muggeridge once likened death to approaching harbour at the end of a voyage. At the beginning of the voyage, he said, we are only interested in whether we will have a cabin with a good porthole, who are the more interesting and attractive passengers and whether we will be asked to sit at the Captain's table. As the harbour comes in sight, he said, all this looks absurd. That, of course, is why some people as they get older and face up to the prospect of death, do indeed begin to reorder their priorities. But for much of our life, and for some even when we get old, we are primarily driven by considerations of personal comfort (whether the cabin has a porthole), by ambition or lust (associating only with the more important and attractive people) and whether the world is sitting up to take notice of us (whether we will be invited to sit at the Captain's table). A state of mind that is driven by such considerations has little use for religion. Religion might occasionally be used, when a parson is given a walk-on part at a daughter's wedding, or a memorial service is arranged for a business colleague, but religion is not allowed into the centre. For religion, by definition, shakes up and reorders our lives. Yet, sometimes, even when we have all we want, something of the divine can break through and touch us. When C. S. Lewis was bereaved he wrote in the notebook which he kept to help him stay sane:

> One thing, however, marriage has done for me. I can never again believe that religion is manufactured out of our unconscious, starved desires and is a substitute for sex. For those few years H. and I feasted on love; every mode of it . . . No cranny of heart or body remained unsatisfied. If God were a substitute for love we ought to have lost all interest in him. Who'd bother about substitutes when he has the thing itself? But that isn't what happens. We both knew we wanted something besides one another – quite a different kind of something, a quite different kind of want.[3]

So, for all that is decent and good in the world, for all that flourishes, whether people acknowledge the divine source or not, the religious believer will give thanks. The person of faith will also acknowledge that they come to God with empty hands held out, as needy. Sometimes they come, as the eucharistic prayer of St Thomas Aquinas puts it, 'As sick to the physician of life'.

There are those who do not feel this need. But in the words of the poem by C. H. Sisson that began this chapter:

> Come down and speak to the men of ability
> On the Sevenoaks platform and tell them
> That at your St Nicholas the faith
> Is not exclusive in the fools it chooses
> That the vain, the ambitious and the highly sexed
> Are the natural prey of the incarnate Christ.

PART 5

Towards a Spirituality for Today

CHAPTER 17

Our True Self

In the coming world they will not ask me: 'Why were you not Moses?'
They will ask me: 'Why were you not Zusya?'

(Rabbi Zusya of Hanipol)

We were born to make manifest the glory of God that is within us. It
is not just in some of us; it is in everyone.

(Nelson Mandela)

I began this book quoting statistics indicating the growing number of
people who see themselves as spiritual without being religious, some of
whom indeed are hostile to traditional religion as they have encountered it.
People in this category cover a broad range of views, from those who
receive their spiritual nourishment through the arts, especially music,
through to those who belong to the movement loosely called New Age.
Steve Bruce, a sociologist who has written widely on secularization and the
role of religion in the modern world, sums up the essence of such spirituality in these words:

> First there is the belief that the self is divine. Christianity always
> assumed a division between God the creator and all the people he
> created. God was good; people were bad . . . The new age does not
> have divisions . . . The point of the spiritual journey is to free the God
> within, to get in touch with our true centre.[1]

That description does, I believe, resonate much more widely than those
who would consciously describe themselves as New Age. It lies behind
many of the objections to traditional religion that have been considered in
this book. I wish now to address this 'spiritual' outlook more directly, for
I believe that Christianity has within its treasure store enormous spiritual

riches – riches which can be made accessible to those who see themselves as spiritual rather than religious, without in any way compromising orthodox Christian doctrine.

'First there is the belief that the self is divine.' It all depends of course on what one means by the 'self' as well as what one means by 'divine'. Christianity does not believe that the clamant ego, the self-preoccupied, grasping motivator of so much of what we do, is divine. Quite the contrary; this is the self that, as St Paul puts it, needs to be crucified with Christ. But St Paul also said that the mystery hidden from the ages and now revealed is 'Christ in you the hope of glory' (Colossians 1.27). Our true self is nothing less than the Christ who is being formed within us. Earlier I quoted the poem by Gerard Manley Hopkins:

> For Christ plays in ten thousand places
> Lovely in limbs and lovely in eyes not his
> To the Father through the features of men's faces.

We can see how this is so by approaching the matter in another way. Moment by moment all that exists springs from God, the fount of all being. But he wills not only to undergird our life but to permeate it and fill it from within. When in union with Christ we turn to and trust God our heavenly Father, a sluice is, as it were, opened in the soul and the Spirit rises to fill us from within. Or to put it the other way round, it is the Spirit that opens that sluice and filling us from within enables us to relate to God our Father. That Spirit who fills us shapes and forms the life of Christ within us. That Christ is nothing less than our soul's soul, our true self. This does not mean the obliteration of our ordinary human characteristics, except for our egotism and ruthless pursuit of our own interests. The characteristic features of our personality, which make us what we are, and by which people recognize us as the person we are, become richer and more distinctive, the more they are transparent to the Christ who is being formed within us. Indeed, what Christianity means by the resurrection of the body is not the gathering together of the physical corpuscles, but the recreation of those distinctive features of our person which make us what we are, in a manner and form appropriate to an eternal existence.

'Christianity always assumed a division between God the creator and all the people he created . . . God was good; and people were bad . . . The new age does not have that division.' There is indeed a division between God and all created existence. God is the underived source of all that exists, the complete and perfect ground of all being. Everything that exists exists solely by his *fiat*. Without his undergirding power and presence the universe would dissolve into the nothingness from which it sprang. Nevertheless, this abyss has been crossed. For God not only wills to hold the universe in being but, as has been said, to fill it with his presence. As the writer to the Ephesians puts it, there is 'One God and Father of all, who is over all and through all and in all' (Ephesians 4.6).

However, the Christian faith says much more than that God dwells in his creation through his Spirit. It is through Jesus Christ that he comes to shape and fill all things. The bridge thrown across the abyss between the uncreated source of all things in creation is the person of Jesus Christ. But through Christ, God works first to fill the Church, and then all things, with his presence. It is this theme which is spelt out so profoundly in the letters to the Colossians and Ephesians.

First, 'For it is in Christ that the complete being of the Godhead dwells embodied' (Colossians 2.9).

Second, the God who fills Christ Jesus wills to fill those who are his. The great prayer in Ephesians ends up, 'That you may be filled with all the fullness of God' (Ephesians 3.19).

Third, the purpose of God does not end there. It is to fill all things with his presence. For the Church is 'His body, the fullness of him who fills all in all' (Ephesians 1.23).

'God was good; people were bad . . . the new age does not have that division . . . the point of the spiritual journey is to free the God within, to get in touch with our true centre.' Christianity's first and fundamental assertion is that the world has been created good. The theme running through the creation story in the book of Genesis is that God saw what he had made and it is good. To use the title of a famous book by Matthew Fox, there is an original blessing. But no one can read the newspapers, watch television or be alive for very long without a stark realization that something, somewhere along the line, has gone badly wrong. This is not simply due to the survival of our animal instincts. It is something that has gone morally wrong of which the holocaust, Stalin's purges, genocide under Pol Pot and in Rwanda and elsewhere, are just some of the unspeakable cruelties which human beings have perpetrated. But in and through Jesus Christ, God comes among us to restore and recreate human life as it should be, a life at one with our Creator and with one another in a mutuality of love. This love is nothing less than God himself dwelling with us and within us. *Ubi caritas et amor Deus ibi est.* God is love, asserts St John's gospel, and we are to share that love, that is share the divine nature. The writer of the second letter of Peter says that the divine power has been bestowed on us 'That you might be partakers of the divine nature' (2 Peter 1.4). This has become the basis of a central theme of Orthodox Christianity, that of *theosis*, or our deification in and through Christ. It is there in the Early Church Fathers such as Irenaeus, who said that as God came to share our life in the incarnation so we are destined to share the divine life and become what he is. It is there in Athanasius who said that 'the Word became flesh that we, partakers of his spirit, might be deified'. It is there in Cyril of Alexandria who asserted that 'He became man that we might become divine'.[2]

There are other ways of putting this truth in the New Testament. St Paul concentrates on the image of son-ship. Through the unique son-ship of Jesus Christ we are to become fully sons and daughters of God. In the Johannine writings the emphasis is upon God coming to dwell within us as we obey the command of Jesus to love one another. The image of *theosis* or deification has been less emphasized in Western Christianity but it speaks directly to those whose spirituality is sympathetic to some of the insights of the new age. Indeed, that spirituality is groping its way towards fundamental truths which are stated more fully, with a proper balance, within the Christian tradition, as I hope I have shown.

The German novelist Herman Hesse wrote, 'When a man tries, with the gifts bestowed on him by nature, to fulfil himself, he is doing the highest thing he can do, the only thing that has any meaning.' This sums up succinctly the dominant idea of the twentieth century. Self-expression and self-fulfilment override all other considerations. This is related to new age spirituality because although conscious adherents to that movement may be relatively small in number, our whole culture is saturated with the idea of the self and its development. People use the concept of self-fulfilment as both their starting point and the criterion by which they judge what is on offer in the way of spirituality and religion. All this of course is not unrelated to the fact that we live in a world dominated by the market economy, with consumer choice being paramount. I do not believe that Christians should simply knock this or dismiss it out of hand. After all, those of us who are parents want our children to fulfil themselves, to develop the potential that they have within them. If we, flawed as we are, want good things for our children, how much more does God, who is perfect, want good things for us, as Jesus pointed out (Matthew 7.11).

A Christian critique should come, not in dismissing the whole idea of self-fulfilment out of hand but by pointing out one obvious truth and posing one question. The obvious truth is that fulfilment in life comes from giving oneself to what is worthwhile. It comes as a by-product of doing something else. We engage in something that interests us, let us say carpentry or gardening, and as a result find fulfilment. If we simply seek fulfilment in itself, it not only eludes but is likely to destroy us. From a Christian point of view, ultimate fulfilment comes through giving ourselves to that which is ultimately worthwhile, of supreme worth, namely God himself. This path is open to all people, of all religions. It is this, I believe, which the growing constituency of self-defined spiritual people is feeling its way towards. William Law (1686–1761), a man of impeccable Christian orthodoxy, wrote:

There is but one salvation for all mankind, and that is the life of God in the soul. God has but one design or interest towards all mankind, and that is to introduce or generate his own life, light and spirit in them, that all may be as so many images, temples and habitations of the Holy Trinity. This is God's will to all Christians, Jews and heathens. They are all equally the desire of his heart. Now there is but one possible way for man to attain this salvation. There is no one way for a Jew, another for a Christian and a third for a heathen. No, God is one, human nature is one, salvation is one, and the way to it is one, and that is the desire of the soul turned to God.

It is in that turning to God of the soul that we release and discover our true self.

The question we pose, one which has already been implicit in this chapter, is what is our true self? The self is not identical with the grasping ego, or the unconscious, nor (with due respect to Jung), the collective unconscious, if there is a such a thing. We are truly ourselves as we allow Christ, through the Holy Spirit, to be formed within us.

This self is, first of all, a gift. There seems to be a universal human tendency to want to assert our superiority over other people. They may be cleverer than we are, but they are socially inferior, they don't belong to the right class. Or they may be socially superior but they don't have the right political or ecclesiastical views. They are not one of us. Or they may be very successful but really they don't have any charisma, they are terribly dull. And so on. The heart is endlessly devious in the way it distances itself from others and puts them down. This is betrayed by the way that so often we are trying to prove ourselves, as though we feel we are inferior and want to show the world the opposite. Or, if you like, we are, in one way if not another, trying to justify ourselves. Sometimes that attempt to justify ourselves takes the form of thinking ourselves as more moral than other people, or more religious.

All this is terribly misconceived and the cause of a great deal of the hatred and violence in the world. For the fact is, our self is sheer gift. It is given us by God in creation and in Jesus Christ is welcomed and gathered to himself. We don't have to prove ourselves, justify ourselves or give a successful performance at anything. We are valuable as we are, loved and cherished by God as ourselves – not as anyone else, but as ourselves.

It was this great truth which was rediscovered at the Reformation and which in recent decades has been rediscovered by the Roman Catholic Church. Our relationship with God does not depend upon giving a successful performance, either moral or religious. 'For it is by his grace you are saved, through trusting him; it is not your own doing. It is God's gift, not a reward for work done' (Ephesians 2.8). This self is both a gift and a process. Through baptism and faith we are already joined to Christ. But the fullness of what we are to become lies ahead.

> Here and now, dear friends, we are God's children; what we shall be has not yet been disclosed, but we know that when it is disclosed we shall be like him, because we shall see him as he is. (1 John 3.2)

This process of becoming our true self is not a lonely, isolated one: it is inseparably linked to our relationships to other people within the body of Christ. It is in the new society reconstituted by God round Jesus that we grow as ourself. It is through mutual vulnerability and interdependence; through the sharing and building up of one another, that the self which is sheer gift develops into the glorious self that shall be; a self bonded and bound up with others in our common life in Christ, the *Koinonia*. A life that is at once life with one another and life in God.

Rowan Williams quotes the words of a spiritual:

> O nobody knows who I am
> Til the judgement morning.

He argues that the truth of this is inseparable first of all from God's vulnerability in Jesus Christ and then from our relationships with one another as we allow people to tell us who we are. 'We shall none of us know who we are without each other – which may mean we shan't know who we are until Judgement Day.'

> We are all to find out who we are in the light of God in Jesus, and that finding *is* the process of living in a community struggling to discover means of mutual empowering and affirming, in the conviction that we shall not live or flourish if we consider any person or group dispensable, or merely functional for our own self definition.[3]

Too often we speak for others and define them in our terms. But the church should be a community in which people speak for themselves and share their pain as well as their hurt. That mutual vulnerability is made possible by the God who has made himself vulnerable to us. It is in that community of mutual hearing, mutual affirming and shared penitence, all made possible because of God's gift to us in Jesus Christ and the hope held out to us, that we grow together into that selfhood, Christ himself, the fullness of him who fills all in all.

CHAPTER 18

Re-creating Humanity

We have to love our crooked neighbour with our crooked heart.
(W. H. Auden)

The incomprehensibility and unknowability of God in himself is not a modern opinion arrived at out of a despair of talking about God at all; it is basic to Christian orthodoxy and needs to be asserted time and again, against all attempts to put God in our philosophical, theological or linguistic pockets. Nevertheless, that said, God *has* chosen to make himself known in a humanly accessible way. As Austin Farrer put it: 'God is in no place, because he contains all places. Only he has gathered himself out of all immensity to lodge himself in the eyes and heart of Jesus: and there we are to find him.'[1]

How are we to grasp or even begin to approach this stupendous truth? Much depends on our starting point. In the same way that the answer you get depends on the kind of question you ask, so that asking the right questions becomes crucial, what we concede to be the fundamental problem about human existence will affect the route we take to try and find an answer.

Gotama Buddha was brought up in a comfortable home protected so far as possible from the miseries of the world. Then he started to travel and discovered people who were ill, old and dying. Suffering seemed to be everywhere. He came to the conclusion that the basic problem of life was the ubiquity of suffering, and therefore the religious quest must, above all, be about finding a way of not being inwardly thrown or overcome by it. So he taught the four noble truths of Buddhism and its eightfold path as a way of achieving an inner serenity that could remain untouched by the anguish that afflicts all life.

Karl Marx took a different view of the problem. It was that the full range of human potential was being blocked because of the industrial revolution, behind which lay the exploitation of one class by another. He looked to a series of primarily economic revolutions until a human society came into being that was free of exploitation and every human being could develop their potential to the full.

While Christianity has points of contact with both Buddhism and Marxism, its starting point is different. It conceives the basic problem of human existence to be not suffering as such or exploitation as such but a radical inability to relate to one another in mutual care. Much, though not all, suffering results from this; and economic exploitation is one, though not the only manifestation of this basic flaw. Cain murdered Abel and ever since then human history has been a record of murders on a small and large scale. Every day in our newspapers or through our radio or television, we learn of terrible things – rape, child abuse, murders, robberies, wars and genocide. The twentieth century, the most advanced that the world has known in terms of scientific and technological progress, saw, among other things, the terrible carnage of the First and Second World Wars, Stalin's purges in which 28 million died, the Holocaust, millions killed under Pol Pot in Cambodia, genocide in Rwanda, as well as a multitude of 'lesser' crime such as the loss of more than a million Armenians in Turkey, the killing of Muslims in Bosnia and Christians in the Moluccas, and so on.

Although the West enjoys an unprecedented high standard of living there is family breakdown on a massive scale, as well as a catalogue of crimes. The problem is simply how we can live together without destroying one another, in the family, the local community, in the nation and between nations. Law has a vital role to play, setting basic minimum standards which people can be coerced into obeying. But it does not get to the heart of the matter. Politics has a vital part as well, achieving skilful comprises. But again, this does not get to the root of conflict.

The purpose of God in creation is to bring about a universal, inclusive society, characterized by a profound mutual care that draws on the depth of love within God himself. Because this purpose is being continually frustrated, something had to be done about it.

Both Judaism and Christianity teach that God himself has set out to tackle this problem. In short, God has acted to re-constitute or re-create human society on a new basis, not just leaving it to us to slug it out until we are exhausted. In order to re-create humanity as a whole he has first of all chosen a particular people, the Jews, that in their communal living, the good life, life as it ought to be, might flourish. To this end he did two things. First, he made a solemn binding promise (a covenant) that he would stick by them through thick and thin. Second, he disclosed to them the basic principles and rules by which society should live, which would bring about the flourishing of all (the Torah).

This twin disclosure did however have one, inevitable consequence. By revealing what God gives to his people and what he wants from them, it also highlights the ways when the community falls short of what is required. So it was that God kept on inspiring particular individuals to recall the community to God's promise and what was required of them, still holding out the hope that true community would one day be realized (the Prophets).

Christianity believes that God's work of re-creating human society on a new basis comes to a focus in Jesus. In a series of vivid pictures he sketched out the kind of society God was creating, the kind of person who would be at home in it, and invited all who would to begin living in it now (the kingdom of God). Furthermore, he gathered around him a group of 12 intimate friends who were to be the nucleus of that new society.

The characteristic feature of this society is that in principle everyone is included. Jesus likened it to a great feast or banquet to which we are all invited, and went out of his way to mix with and eat with groups of whom respectable society disapproved. Jesus saw himself as gathering people into this new world. At one stage he lamented over Jerusalem that it had murdered the messengers God sent to it: 'How often have I longed to gather your children, as a hen gathers her brood under her wings; but you would not let me' (Matthew 23.37).

At one stage he wept over Jerusalem, foreseeing what would happen to it because it did not know the things that make for peace.

The mission of Jesus ended in apparent failure. The new community he had created disintegrated as his closest followers fled. Yet not long afterwards they came together convinced that, contrary to all appearances, God had won a decisive victory over evil and that his work continued – not in a vague way but quite specifically in and through Jesus, the icon of God. For he continues to give shape and definition to the act of God first initiated in the people of Israel and now coming to a focus in his life, death and resurrection.

His followers, now beginning to be joined by others, saw themselves as the new society inaugurated by Jesus; indeed, a new humanity. The solemn, binding promise which God had made with the people of Israel, to be with them through thick and thin, had been reaffirmed, especially through the death of Jesus, which now made it possible for anyone, however burdened by their past, to take their place at a special meal which was a feature of the new community. In short, human society was re-created around Jesus who lives both beyond death as head of the new community and in and through his followers, who form his continuing body in history.

The New Testament makes staggering claims about Jesus which, particularly in the fourth gospel, are set out in a range of images. Here I take just one, that of light. In an art gallery it is important for the paintings to be well displayed and appropriately lit so that viewers can see them to best advantage. Light reveals the painting as it is, as it is meant to be seen. Light also has another function: it can reveal dust and cobwebs. It not only reveals things as they are but discloses what might otherwise remain hidden. Rays of a special wavelength, X-rays, can even reveal what is going on inside our bodies. According to the synoptic gospels, Jesus taught the coming of a time of total exposure: 'For there is nothing hidden that will not become public, nothing under cover that will not be made known and brought into the open' (Luke 8.17). He said to one group of people:

> There is nothing covered up that will not be uncovered, nothing hidden that will not be made known. You may take it, then, that everything you have said in the dark will be heard in broad daylight, and what you have whispered behind closed doors will be shouted from the house-tops. (Luke 12.2, 3)

In St John's gospel Jesus himself is the light in which everything is seen and in which everything is exposed:

> Here lies the test: the light has come into the world, but men preferred darkness to light because their deeds were evil. Bad men all hate the light and avoid it, for fear their practices should be shown up. The honest man comes to the light so that it may be clearly seen that God is in all he does. (John 3.19–21)

This exposure to the light of truth implies accountability. The concept of accountability can seem negative, even threatening. But take the example of two undergraduates returning home after their first term at university. In one home the parents made no inquiry about how their daughter got on. In the other they take a real interest. They ask how she got on with her work, her friends and her other interests. In this second home the daughter gives an account of her life at college. As she gives an account she realizes that during her first term she has in fact spent a great deal of time chatting to her friends and not much time working. It is because her parents took an interest in what she was doing, cared about it, that in rendering an account of herself she saw a truth that she might otherwise have resisted. In the first home there was indifference; in the second there was love. It is this love that leads to an account being given – in response to the question 'How did you get on?' – and this in turn allows truths to dawn. At the same time, in this second home there is an overwhelming assurance, mostly unstated, because it can be so assumed, that the daughter has a place in that home, is a member of the family. So it is that the dawning of the light of truth is inseparably connected to a love which takes an interest in us and a love which assures us of a place in the home. Home is where they have to take you in, as a poet put it. Even if that daughter had got into terrible trouble, she was assured that she had a place in her home.

In the end all will be known. The light of divine truth will reveal everything for what it is, exposing what is hidden and disclosing the inmost secrets of the heart. At the same time, this light is love, a love who out of love asks us how we got on with our lives. In telling our story the truth, at once gentle and searing, will dawn upon us.

All this belongs to the end, to God himself. But the New Testament makes the claim that this end has come near, has come close to us in Jesus. He is that light and love before whom we are now exposed, to whom we can tell our story and who assures us of our place in his new society. That light is the one which will, in the end, illuminate and reveal all things.

Now we are assured that we have a place in the new society, a place at table in the eucharistic feast.

The first Christians believed that their community was God's reconstitution of society in embryo. In the Acts of the Apostles we have a moving description of their life together. Scholars suggest that this may present a somewhat idealized picture, but at the very least it represents the ideal to which they aspired.

> They met constantly to hear the apostles teach, and to share the common life, to break bread, and to pray. A sense of awe was everywhere, and many marvels and signs were brought about through the apostles. All whose faith had drawn them together held everything in common: they would sell their property and possessions and make a general distribution as the need of each required. With one mind they kept up their daily attendance at the temple, and, breaking bread in private houses, shared their meals with unaffected joy, as they praised God and enjoyed the favour of the whole people. And day by day the Lord added to their number those whom he was saving. (Acts 2.41–47)

Three features of this new society are pertinent to my theme, which I take first from the writings of St Paul. First, it is to be characterized by mutual love. Paul wrote that 'The whole law is summed up in love' (Romans 13.10), and 1 Corinthians 13 contains his famous hymn to love which ends up: 'In a word, there are three things that last for ever: faith, hope and love; but the greatest of them all is love.'

In the next chapter he goes on to talk about spiritual gifts in the church, but he begins that chapter with the words 'Put love first'. In his letters he deals with a whole range of pastoral issues. Love is his guiding principle and it is this he urges on his congregations.

Second, this mutual love means that the very concept of self-hood becomes stretched to include the other. We see this in Paul's own identification with the struggles and suffering of his fellow Christians. 'If anyone is weak, do I not share his weakness? If anyone is made to stumble, does my heart not blaze with indignation?' (2 Corinthians 11.29). In a famous image he likens the Christian Church to a body in which each limb has its own specialist function but in which there is total mutual interdependence. 'If one organ suffers, they all suffer together. If one flourishes they all rejoice together' (1 Corinthians 12.26).

Third, this growth in mutual love, this building up of one another, is at the same time the growth of Christ in us. In the letter to the Ephesians quoted earlier the writer says that Christ has given everyone in the Church their own particular charism, or gift of the Spirit, and this is:

> To equip God's people for work in his service, to the building up of the body of Christ. So shall we all at last attain to the unity inherent in our faith and our knowledge of the Son of God – to mature manhood, measured by nothing less than the full stature of Christ. (Ephesians 4.12, 13)

In short, as Christians use their particular gifts for the service of God, the body of Christ is built up. This brings about mature manhood, or what today we would call mature humanity. But the definition of humanity is not a secular one: it is defined and measured by Christ in his fullness, that fullness including his body as it more and more reflects his life and is filled with his Spirit.

These same three truths are stated with great force and clarity in the central sections of St John's gospel (John 13.31—17.26). Like a refrain or theme in a piece of music it recurs with slight variations time and again. The theme is that if we love Christ we are to obey him, and what he asks of us is that we love one another. If we love one another then he himself and his Father will come and dwell within us. This indwelling will bring forth fruit which will make the disclosure of God in Christ known to others.

Those first Christians believed that what was happening in their own communal life would one day happen to the whole universe. For God was reconstituting human society around Jesus and in the end Jesus would be seen to be Lord of all. In his discussion of resurrection where Paul sees the resurrection of Jesus as the firstfruit of the resurrection of all the dead, he paints a picture of the end in these words:

> Then comes the end, when he delivers up the kingdom to God the Father, after abolishing every kind of domination, authority and power. For he is destined to reign until God has put all enemies under

his feet; and the last enemy to be abolished is death . . . then the Son himself will also be made subordinate to God who made all things subject to him, and thus God will be all in all. (1 Corinthians 15.24–28)

This reminds us that the new society being created by God has its fulfilment beyond space and time. Because it is a human society it has to be built up on this earth, but because it is also a divine society it cannot be limited to this earth or trapped by space and time. It is a human/divine society formed around Jesus in his incarnation but risen, ascended and glorified with him to live in God for ever. It is also what we call the Communion of Saints. Popular piety focuses on particularly holy or outstanding individuals, but this is only part of the truth. It is a *communion* of saints. It is a communion of people bonded and knit together in love, suffused and filled with the divine love made manifest in Jesus, irradiated by the glory of God in every aspect. The Communion of Saints bears out the great truth which can be discovered in this life, that the greater the mutuality of love, the more distinctive and rich is each individual life. Western society has been shaped for too long by the totally distorted notion that we develop our self by separation from others and asserting our individuality. It is precisely the opposite which is true. It is as we give ourselves to others in love, building them up, that our own growth in self-hood takes place, secretly, mysteriously and yet obvious to others. The greater the unity of love, the greater the richness of the selves that contribute to and receive from that mutuality. It is this process that comes to its climax and consummation within the Communion of Saints.

The truth of this can be seen from a number of different points of view. First, as a matter of straightforward fact, mind is a social reality. We see mothers bending over their pram and making noises at the baby inside. In due course that baby begins to make similar noises. Soon the noise turns into recognizable sounds and the baby learns to talk. That talking goes on inside him in what we call thinking. In short, we are talked into talking and talked into that talking inside us that we term thinking. There is no such thing as a totally isolated individual. We become minds and persons only in and through our relationships with other minds and other persons.

The novelist and theological writer Charles Williams saw this mutuality developing in our willingness to recognize and appreciate the qualities of others, and wrote a poem using the image of heaven as a great wedding feast:

He saw along
the Great Hall and the Heavenly Stair
one blaze of glorious changes there.
Cloaks, broaches, decorations, swords,
jewels – every virtue that affords
(by dispensation of the throne)
beauty to wearers not their own.
This guest his brother's courage wore;
that, his wife's zeal, while, just before,
she in his steady patience shone;
there a young lover had put on
the fine integrity of sense
his mistress used; magnificence
a father borrowed of his son,
who was not there ashamed to don
his father's wise economy.
No he or she was he or she
merely no single being dared
except the Angels of the Guard
come without other kind of dress
than his poor life had to profess,
and yet those very robes were shown,
when from preserval as his own
into another's glory given,
bright ambiguities of heaven.[2]

This is what Charles Williams called the way of exchange, whereby we take on and take into ourselves the qualities developed by other people while they, in their turn, take on and take into themselves the qualities which we have developed. This is a truth that has too long been lost in Western society but still preserved, for example, in Africa. Whereas the West is dominated by Descartes' 'I think therefore I am', in African traditional society the prevailing ethos is that of ubuntu, 'I am with others, therefore I am'.

The first Christian community experienced this life in a remarkable way, a way which seemed to break down all traditional barriers. One of the strongest that they were conscious of was that between Jews and Gentiles. But in the new order of things, human society reconstituted around Jesus, this old division fell away.

Gentiles and Jews, he has made the two one, and in his own body of flesh and blood has broken down the enmity which stood like a dividing wall between them; for he annulled the law with its rules and regulations, so as to create out of the two a single new humanity in himself, thereby making peace. (Ephesians 2.14–15)

We note from this passage that it is not just society which is being re-created but humanity in all its aspects.

All this is a wonderful ideal. Then we come to a juddering halt before the reality of the Church as it has appeared in history and as we might have experienced it ourselves. Too often in history the Church has seemed simply to reflect the prevailing outlook of society, very often its worst aspects. Too often the life of individual congregations now can seem mean and petty-minded. If the Early Church saw itself as the new human/divine society in embryo, the Church in history has hardly looked like that. Too often the Church has seemed not a sign of the kingdom of God but as just one more expression of human divisiveness, our congenital incapacity to relate to one another. This is a point we need to look straight in the face without any attempts to evade or sidestep the terrible indictment that can be made. What can be said on the other side? First, although the ideal is constantly held out by the New Testament writers, they were all too conscious of human failures. There are as many failures recorded about the Early Church in the New Testament as in any Church anywhere. Nor did this just concern the congregations to whom Paul was writing, trying to get them to sort out their differences and difficulties. It happened to Paul himself. For example, Paul and Barnabas quarrelled about whether to take John Mark with them on a missionary journey. Mark had let them down before and Paul refused to take him. 'The dispute was so sharp that they parted company. Barnabas took Mark with him and sailed for Cyprus, while Paul chose Silas' (Acts 15.39). This brings out the second point. What did hold and does hold Christians together is certainly not perfection of life. It is that, despite everything, we are accepted by God and on this basis accept one another with all our faults and failings. 'In a word, accept one another as Christ accepted us, to the glory of God' (Romans 15.7).

This truth is rooted in the teaching and example of Jesus and is absolutely fundamental to our whole understanding of how community is created and what holds it together. For central to the teaching of Jesus is what he said about forgiveness: God's forgiveness of us and our forgiveness of other people. These two are integrally tied together (Matthew 6.14, 25; Matthew 18.23–35). This teaching, stated so strongly in parable and injunction, is a crucial part of the Lord's Prayer. Daily Christians pray 'Father, forgive our sins as we forgive those who sin against us'. Forgiveness is not some mechanical wiping of the slate clean. It is continuing to relate to someone and to care for them even though you feel they have done you some wrong. It is holding someone in a costly, painful relationship. Christianity has always taken the dark side of human nature seriously. Therefore it has always resisted the possibility of man-made utopias on this earth. For although there can be progress and improvements in many ways, in every good there is a seed of evil. The only hope therefore is for a community that takes this fully into account and has, as it were, a built-in remedy. That remedy is a holding of one another in relationship, a relationship which is grounded in God's relationship to us. God's relationship to us is sheer gift, all grace. It is from this that the possibility of holding others in relationship, despite all hurts, can grow. This means that the Christian community will always be characterized by both a sense of penitence, of falling short of what we could be, together with an assurance that we are held in God's love and can continue in the community and where there is always a seat for us at the table.

One third point needs to be made. Those of us who continue as members of the Christian community do so because we have caught some glimpse, however fragmentary, of what it is meant to be. It may be that we have been inspired by someone of conspicuous goodness or holiness, whose life was inspired by Christ. It may be that we have belonged to a congregation or community that clearly had something very distinctive and special about it in the way of care and spiritual depth. Unless one had had some experience like this, then one would not have remained a member of the Church. It is because of such experiences that people are able to survive periods of disillusionment when the Christian Church seems to lack all credibility.

A key text for understanding the new society which Jesus came to bring into being comes from the first letter of John:

> Our theme is the word of life. This life was made visible; we have seen it and bear our testimony; we here declare to you the eternal life which dwelt with the father and was made visible to us. What we have seen and heard we declare to you, so that you and we together may share in a common life, that life which we share with the Father and his son Jesus Christ. (1 John 1.2, 3)

This passage makes it clear that the Christian community emerges in history in response to the divine life made visible in Jesus. The Church proclaims this message: 'What we have seen and heard we declare to you.' But this message is not simply to be heard, it is set forth in order that people might be drawn into the Christian community. It is 'So that you and we together may share in a common life.' But that common life is not just that of any human grouping. It is 'That life which we share with the Father and his son Jesus Christ.' The word translated here as 'common life', which is repeated twice, both in relation to the life which we have with one another and the life which we share with God, is *Koinonia*. This has become an important word in all the churches in recent decades. It has been to the fore in relationships between different churches, for it highlights the fact that whatever divisions there may be there is a common life, a life in Christ, a communion in which we are held together. It is also a word that has become important within the Anglican Communion, holding together those who have been divided over the issue of the ordination of women to the priesthood. What is fundamental and so wonderful about this word is that it takes us into the very life of God himself. It is the life of mutual love within the blessed Trinity, that life which was disclosed to us in the relationship between Jesus and the one he called *Abba*, Father; a life made possible by the Holy Spirit that, flowing from the Father, filled him. It is into this life that, through Christ, we are taken.

The Church therefore does not consist of a loose association of people who happen to have something called religion or the Christian faith in common. Members of a congregation may not have much in common. They may like or dislike one another. Some may be friends and others not. All this is beside the point. The point is that as Christians they belong to one another in Christ, rooted and grounded in his love and on the basis of that accepting one another and seeking to build one another up.

To sum up. The purpose of God and creation is to bring about a universal, inclusive society characterized by a profound mutual care that draws on the depths of love within God himself. This points up the fact that the fundamental problem of human existence is our disastrous failure to live amicably with one another. In response to this tragic state of affairs God has acted to re-create human society, to re-constitute it round Jesus, who gives shape and definition to God's continuing actions in the world. The Christian community is the embryo of this new human/divine society, which one day will encompass and transfigure all things. It is in this community that, through love, through building one another up in the service of God and others, we discover our true self. This self is with others, not apart from them. It is also nothing less than the life of God within us, reflecting the mutual giving and receiving of the blessed Trinity.

CHAPTER 19

On Not Saying Too Much

Church gradually became a place of torment to me. For there men dared to preach aloud – I am tempted to say, shamelessly – about God, about his intentions and actions. There people were exhorted to have those feelings and to *believe* that secret which I *knew* to be the deepest, innermost certainty, a certainty not to be betrayed by a single word. I could only conclude that apparently no one knew about this secret, not even the parson, for otherwise no one would have dared to expose the mystery of God in public and to proclaim those inexpressible feelings with stale sentimentalities.

(C. G. Jung)[1]

Jung was a parson's son. He knew the religious scene from inside. His profound sense of the ultimate mystery of God made him react strongly against the pat way the divine purpose was talked about. 'I grew more and more sceptical, and my father's sermons and those of other parsons became acutely embarrassing to me.' With all that we know about the unfathomable mystery of the universe today, for anyone with any religious sensitivity that reaction against any view of God that comes across as over-assured, cocky and having things all tied up, will be even more acute.

When we contemplate the universe in which we live, the mind literally boggles. The imagination is stretched beyond that with which it can cope. Evolution has occurred over billions of years, with *homo sapiens* emerging only in the last few seconds of the evolutionary clock. Countless species have lived and died out. Now, here we are, with our momentary blink of life. The universe is expanding with an amazing velocity. When we send up space probes to, say, Mars we are only exploring the edge of our own solar system, which is but a speck of dust in the vast void exploding ever away from us. When we consider the human body we now know through the discovery of DNA how it is organized by literally millions of chemical reactions.

We gain some purchase on all this through the language of mathematics, physics and genetics. We explore the microcosm and discover strange entities called quarks. We grope into the outer reaches of the universe and label even more mysterious entities as black holes. The human genome project has already mapped all the genes in the human body. But the actual reality of that which science sketches out confronts us with its sheer, impenetrable 'isness'. Through the miracle of the human mind we can know something about the universe with the aid of the language of science. But in the end there is a baffling quality about that which is before us; that which makes us gasp and wonder, even become awe-struck.

If the universe strikes us in this way, blowing the mind, how much more appropriate is this sense when contemplating a creator of it. That is why, when religious people give the impression that God and his ways are all buttoned up, when they talk in a familiar, cocky way, without any sense of the unfathomable nature of that to which they refer, anyone with any sensitivity to the actual nature of the world in which we live draws away. As Jung felt, communication with such people is not possible. In their babbling on they have somehow missed the whole point.

Nor is it fundamentalism that is necessarily at fault here. Fundamentalism has its appalling features, but a sense of the ultimate mystery of the divine is not necessarily one of them. Liberal theology is as prone as any other to falling into the trap. At the height of the *Honest to God* controversy in the 1960s, when the then Bishop of Woolwich, John Robinson, was arguing for a new image of God, a cartoon appeared in *Private Eye*. A preacher was seen proclaiming that 'God is not an old man in the sky with a long beard'. Above the pulpit in the sky was an old man with a long white beard looking down and saying, 'How does he know?'

John of Damascus who lived in the eighth century was not only himself impeccably orthodox but he has long been taken as a standard of orthodoxy, particularly for the Eastern Church. He wrote, 'It is plain, then, that there is a God. But what he is in his essence and nature is absolutely incomprehensible and unknowable.'[2]

Even more influential than John of Damascus have been the works attributed to Dionysius the Areopagite. According to the Acts of the Apostles one of the people who responded positively to the preaching of Paul in Athens was called Dionysius. In the fifth century a body of writings arose which was attributed to this Dionysius. Not only have they been extraordinarily influential in both the East and the West, they have an amazingly modern feel about them when read today. For their concern is with what can and, no less important, what cannot be said about God. Dionysius wrote:

Indeed the inscrutable one is out of the reach of every rational process. Nor can any words come up to the inexpressible Good, this One, this Source of all unity, this supra-existent being. Mind beyond mind, word beyond speech, it is gathered up by no discourse, by no intuition, by no name. It is and it is as no other being is. Cause of all existence, and therefore itself transcending existence, it alone could give an authoritative account of what it really is.[3]

Now, as Dionysius goes on to argue, Christianity does purport to say something true about God. When the word 'mystery' is used in the New Testament, it not only suggests what is beyond the comprehension of the human mind but what has been disclosed to us in Christ. Indeed, St Paul writes, 'The mystery hidden for ages and generations but now made manifest to his saints . . . the riches of the glory of this mystery, which is Christ in you, the hope of glory' (Colossians 1.26–27).

The emphasis in the New Testament is on the fact that this ultimate mystery has been disclosed to us. But it is important to bear in mind the fact that this disclosure comes out of ultimate mystery. In the ancient world there were many mystery religions, some of which anticipated Christianity in offering identification with a God who died and rose again. In contrast to the public, state-sponsored religions which everyone observed as a matter of civic duty, people fulfilled their deepest spiritual needs by belonging to one of these mystery cults. In some respects Christianity would have looked to an outsider like one of these mystery cults, and certainly St Paul did not hesitate to appropriate some of their language. The purpose of the language of revealed religion is not to describe God, who is indescribable: it is to help us to relate truly to that ultimate mystery. Jesus calls us to rethink our whole life (repent), to trust, as though we were trusting the most perfectly conceivable human father, and to follow him in the way of love inspired by his continuing Spirit who dwells within us.

One of the ways in which this truth has been preserved is through the *Via Negativa* or the Apophatic Way. This stresses that everything we say about God positively must at the same time be qualified and denied. We must seek inner purification and wait upon God's wordless love. Another way of putting it, that of the great Anglican theologian Austin Farrer, is that every image of God must be broken then remade, then broken again endlessly.

Christians have disputed bitterly and divisively over words. Words do matter, for by them the truth is preserved. To say that everything we say about God is metaphorical is not the same as saying that one metaphor is as useful as any other. Particular metaphors have particular purposes in particular contexts. For God has indeed disclosed to us true things. But Hilary of Poitiers gets it right when he writes:

The errors of heretics and blasphemers force us to deal with unlawful matters, to scale perilous heights, to speak unutterable words, to trespass on forbidden ground. Faith ought in silence to fulfil the commandments, worshipping the Father, reverencing with him the Son, abounding in the Holy Spirit . . . The error of others compels us to err in daring to embody in human terms truths which ought to be hidden in the silent veneration of the heart.[4]

None of this should be confused with agnosticism, though some forms of agnosticism can have the quality of humility before an ultimately unfathomable divine mystery. To say that God is incomprehensible is not to say that he cannot be truly believed in and responded to. As the poet Gerard Manley Hopkins wrote to his friend Robert Bridges, 'What you mean by a mystery is an interesting uncertainty. What I mean is an incomprehensible certainty.'

If Christianity today is to avoid giving the impression that it is all too pat, too tied up, then this means not only being careful about the use of words, but taking seriously the very real questions and objections people feel about the possibility of believing at all. Donald MacKinnon's inaugural lecture at Cambridge was entitled 'The Borderlands of Theology'. In it he argued that a theologian today must live on the borderlands, feeling the incursions from the other side of the country of belief. His point is fundamental to the whole approach of this book. It will mean that if Christians have a confidence about their faith, it will be a confidence that has a particular quality about it, not dogmatism but a quiet conviction that can coexist with a full apprehension of all the arguments against the maintained position. A review in *The Times Literary Supplement* was headlined on the front page: 'What's wrong with Roger Scruton?'[5] The reviewer Eric Griffiths argued among other things that it was Scruton's dogmatic certainty about aesthetic, moral and religious judgements. He contrasted T. S. Eliot, whom no one could accuse of being vague about his Christian faith, who wrote 'My own beliefs are held with a scepticism which I never even hope to be quite rid of.' That is an interesting sentence. Eliot states that his own beliefs are held with a scepticism and he never even hopes to be quite rid of this scepticism. This suggests a double meaning: one that the scepticism is so deeply ingrained that Eliot recognizes the extreme unlikelihood of him ever eliminating it from his own outlook; the other is that he recognizes the importance of such scepticism, which is why he never even hopes to see it disappear.

In literature of all kinds we distinguish what is genuine from propaganda. What is genuine will usually contain an element of ambiguity. The Argentinian poet Louis Borgès stressed the essential ambiguity at the heart of every work of art and wrote that 'The imminence of a revelation that does not take place is, perhaps, the aesthetic fact.' One of the ways in which Ian McEwan's novel *Enduring Love* fails is that this essential ambiguity is lost. In the novel he depicts an obsessive love by a religious fanatic. The novel ends with this man being hospitalized, complete with an alleged psychiatric case history of this unusual illness. Dante has sometimes been criticized for putting his enemies in hell, but Dante never loses the essential ambiguity, for those whom he depicts in hell very often have noble qualities. McEwan, by simply diagnosing a person's religion as a form of illness, without qualification, and putting that person in hospital, loses any trace of ambiguity. The fact is that the character in the novel might have been at once ill and at the same time expressive of a genuinely enduring love. If religion has too often failed by coming across as no more than a party political broadcast, the secular caste of mind in the modern world often fails as well, through an unwillingness or inability to comprehend what it is for which religion really stands. Two poets who really understood what it is that religious truth could not and should not say were Emily Dickinson and W. H. Auden. In 1868 Emily Dickinson wrote:

> Tell all the truth but tell it slant –
> Success in circuit lies
> Too bright for our infirm delight
> The truth superb surprise
> As lightning to the children of Eve
> With explanation kind
> The truth must dazzle gradually
> Or every man be blind.[6]

W. H. Auden wrote a poem whose title was a quotation from elswhere, 'The Truest Poetry is the Most Feigning', which accurately sums up its theme. He ends by describing the ambiguous nature of human beings, 'Imago Dei who forgot his station', and asks the question:

> What but tall tales, the luck of verbal playing,
> Can trick his lying nature into saying
> That love, or truth in any serious sense,
> Like Orthodoxy, is a reticence?[7]

Emily Dickinson knew that the deepest truths had to be hinted at and suggested, told obliquely. W. H. Auden knew that serious truth and true Orthodoxy is also a reticence. Many people who would not describe themselves as religious instinctively feel this. So do many of those who are feeling their way along the path of spiritual truth but who are put off by the clichés and banalities of so much conventional religion.

Religious belief is itself a thoroughly mysterious phenomenon. How is it, for example, that I believe and several million do not? For a believer their faith comes, in the end, from the Spirit of God himself. St Paul, in writing about God's hidden wisdom, his secret purpose to bring us to our full glory, continues:

> The powers that rule the world have never known it. If they had, they would not have crucified the Lord of glory. But, in the words of Scripture, 'Things beyond our seeing, things beyond our hearing, things beyond our imagining, all prepared by God for those who love him', these it is that God has revealed to us through the Spirit.
>
> For the Spirit explores everything, even the depth of God's own nature. Among men, who knows what a man is but the man's own spirit within him? In the same way, only the Spirit of God knows what God is. This is the Spirit that we have received from God and not the spirit of the world, so that we may know all that God of his own grace has given us. (1 Corinthians 2.8–13)

The question of course arises as to why that Spirit of God does not touch and draw everyone into faith, a question which was pursued further in the chapter on favouritism (Chapter 6). The theme here is the responsibility of those of us who do believe to convey not only the self-disclosure of God in Jesus Christ, but the ultimate mystery of the divine being. It may be that we are now in a time in which religious words and phrases have been so overused and so cheapened that we are called to silence. Certainly this is what Dietrich Bonhoeffer believed. While in prison for his role in the assassination plot on Hitler he wrote 'Thoughts on the baptism of D.W. R.':

> Today you are being baptised as a Christian. The ancient words of the Christian proclamation will be uttered over you, and the command of Jesus to baptise will be performed over you, without your knowing anything about it. But we too are being driven back to first principles. Atonement and redemption, regeneration, the Holy Ghost, the love of our enemies, the cross and resurrection, life in Christ and Christian discipleship – all these things have become so problematic and so remote that we hardly dare anymore to speak of them . . . So our traditional language must perforce become powerless and remain silent and our Christianity today will be confined to praying for and doing right by our fellow men . . . But the day will come when men will be called again to utter the word of God with such power as will change and renew the world . . . Until then the Christian cause will be a silent and hidden affair, but there will be those who pray and do right and wait for God's own time.[8]

That was written in the 1940s, but its truth is even more apparent today. The future belongs to those who pray and do right and wait for God's own time. Canon John Fenton, in an address to ordinands on the St Albans and Oxford Ministry Course, said:

> What the Church will need as its priests is men and women who know that the important and obvious thing about God is that he is silent. He does not speak. He does not grunt, or shuffle his feet, or cough, or do anything to assure us he is there. He meets us in his silence.
>
> The last words of Jesus in Mark's gospel are: My God, my God, why have you forsaken me? He has been given nothing to say. It had all been given to Pilate, the soldiers, the chief priests, the scribes, the passers-by and the centurion; they said who he was, mocking him in unbelief. He was silent, and Pilate was amazed. God was silent, and Jesus was desolate. This is the way.
>
> What the Church needs is people who believe in shutting up; that God is not a talking God; that we do not have the word of God, we have the silence of God. That's all there is, and that's what makes us tick; that's what we want to bring others into.
>
> The purpose of Christian talk is to get us to stop talking.

CHAPTER 20

The Silence of God

If only God would send me some clear sign – like a numbered account
in a Swiss bank.

(Woody Allen)

> O Sabbath rest by Galilee!
> O calm of hills above,
> Where Jesus knelt to share with thee
> The silence of eternity
> Interpreted by love!
>
> ('Dear Lord and Father of Mankind'
> by John Whittier, 1807–92)

For many people the fundamental problem about religious belief is that
there seems no sign of God. It's not just that the philosophical arguments
for or against the existence of God remain inconclusive; it is that they have
no sense of the divine presence and sometimes a great feeling of divine
absence. If God really existed, then surely he would make his presence
more obvious? Certainly, that's what we all sometimes think. As Ludovic
Kennedy put it, 'If he is as real to Christians as he would seem to be, why,
as Bertrand Russell asked, doesn't he make himself known to the rest of
us?'

This problem seems particularly acute in the modern world, for in the
past people have been only too ready to interpret events in terms of divine
action. There is a startling example of this recorded in the New Testament.
Paul cured a man who had been lame from birth:

> When the crowd saw what Paul had done, they shouted, in their
> native Lycaonian, 'The gods have come down to us in human form.'
> And they called Barnabas Jupiter and Paul they called Mercury,

because he was the spokesman. And the priest of Jupiter, whose temple was just outside the city, brought oxen and garlands to the gate, and he and all the people were about to offer sacrifice. (Acts 14.11–13)

There are still parts of the world today which are extraordinarily credulous – the United States of America for example, where many people are willing to believe the most extraordinary things on the basis of no evidence at all. But for many of the rest of us, particularly in Western Europe, there is a deeply suspicious attitude towards interpreting anything in terms of divine presence.

The consciousness of the absence of God can be particularly acute at certain times. For example, when we are besieged with stories on the media of human suffering from all around the world, when innocent people are being slaughtered as they were in Bosnia and Kosovo and East Timor or when millions of young children are dying of AIDS as they are in parts of Africa, the world simply seems devoid of God. Again, it is not a question of the intellectual problem of evil and how this is to be reconciled with belief in the loving God, though that is clearly part of it. It is that, whatever intellectual justification might be given, even if it seems partially persuasive, the world just feels empty.

Nor does it have to be a particular tragedy which brings about this sense. When the poet Edwin Muir was a young man he worked for a period in a Glasgow bone factory. One day, travelling back from work in a bus, he looked across at the people seated opposite him, and they suddenly seemed to be just animals, meat and bones and nothing more. The experience devastated him. A similar sense of horror underlies the writings of Jonathan Swift, the satirist Dean of St Patrick's, Dublin. In our own time it is the writings of Samuel Beckett which have perhaps conveyed this impression more powerfully than most. Beckett's writings have a strong sense of pathos and pity, as well as humour. Nor may they be as devoid of hope as some people might think. But as with that experience of Edwin Muir, there is a consciousness of human beings drained of all sense of spirit, of all divine glory. They are flesh and blood struggling, somehow, just to get through.

For a religious person, someone who has perhaps at some point been conscious of the divine presence, for whom prayer has been a part of their life, there can be a great absence, with prayer seeming totally unreal. At such times in particular we need to question what it is that we really mean by divine presence. What would we allow to count for or against the reality of that presence? Simone Weil once wrote, 'God can only be present in creation under the form of absence.' The most obvious sense in which this is true is that God is not a thing in the world of things, an object among other objects. Any reality that can be categorized in this way could not, by definition, be

God. God is the source and origin of all that is, upholding, enfolding and filling his universe but not identical with any one aspect of it, not a particular but the origin in which and from which all particulars have their existence. That is why it is best to avoid the phrase 'God exists' altogether. For the very word 'existence' can imply existence as we know existence, just one thing among others. God does not exist in that sense. God simply is.

This means that so long as we are looking for God in the form of an isolatable reality, we are not looking for God at all. But when we are conscious of the absence of God conceived in human terms, then we may be on the way to becoming aware of God. As Simone Weil puts it, absence is the form under which God is present in his creation.

There are other ways that this truth can be approached. One of them is in answer to the question why God has created us as part of a physical universe. He could presumably have simply conjured us into being as disembodied spirits, as angels. We wonder why we are flesh and blood, with all the ills that flesh is heir to. The most persuasive answer to this question is that the material world provides, as it were, a screen between us and God. If we were created in the immediate presence of God, we would have no freedom of manoeuvre. We would be like moths drawn inexorably to a candle flame, or filings to a magnet. But because God wants us to have genuine freedom he creates us at a distance from himself. Not, of course, a physical distance, because God is closer to us than we are to ourselves: but what has been called an epistemic distance, a distance of knowing. In other words, we are born into this world with no overwhelming sense of the divine presence. We can only grow in the knowledge and love of God insofar as we are willing to do this, step by step. There are insights and glimmers of light. We grope and feel our way forward. This may feel very unsatisfactory but it serves a prime purpose of safeguarding our freedom. Our spiritual journey is our journey. An ancient Jewish story makes the point in a characteristically vivid way. It depicts God contemplating creating the universe. But he is aware that if he creates it he will fill it with his presence, and all creatures will be overwhelmed, without any true independence. So he lifts up his skirts in order to make a space from which he is absent. That space from which he is absent is the world in which we live, a world in which we can shape our own lives and make our own way towards the divine presence. We are actively to seek:

> Ask, and you will receive; seek and you will find; knock, and the door will be opened. For everyone who asks receives, he who seeks finds, and to him who knocks the door will be opened. (Matthew 7.7)

This seeking must be of a particular kind. It cannot be simply disinterested curiosity. For God is by definition a reality who makes a total difference to our lives. We can only know God the creator of the universe if at the same time we know ourselves to be a creature, as dependent upon this reality as we are upon breathing. So the seeking must be not only an openness to the possibility of faith, but a humility in the face of a disclosing, potentially life-changing reality.

The notion of the absence of God and the silence of God is deeply embedded in the Christian mystical tradition. This is in part because of the acute awareness in that tradition of the limitations of human language. All human words mislead as much as they lead us to God. Therefore, in order to know God, we may have to go into a 'cloud of unknowing'. No less important is the emphasis upon inner purification. Most of what we do is motivated by self-interest of various kinds. Although self-interest can, paradoxically, take us some way to God, because God is our greatest happiness, in order to know God more fully this has to be purged and purified. For if God is total self-giving it is only as we ourselves learn to give of ourselves that we can know him more deeply.

We also have to ask what it means for God to be personal. Thinking of God as personal is encouraged by the Church, which stresses that God 'addresses' us, and that we can bring our requests to him and he will hear them. Faced with the fact that we can see no one, hear no one and that, very often, nothing very much seems to happen in response to our request, it's not surprising that people become more aware of God's absence that his presence. It's important to realize therefore that even when – and especially when – we are conceiving of God in personal terms, we are using metaphor. God is personal in the sense that what we mean by being personal is a faint reflection of personhood within the Godhead. And God is certainly not impersonal or less than personal. Nevertheless, in order to avoid crude misconceptions, it is always important to qualify language that emphasizes the personal nature of God, with impersonal images. The Bible often does this.

Then, while it is true that God seeks to draw us into a relationship with himself, it is no less true that he wishes to dwell within us and calls us to dwell within him. These are metaphors indicating a very different kind of relationship. If it is true that there can be an 'I–thou' relationship with God, it is just as true to say that he dwells within us and we can dwell within him. These are spatial images, rather than ones drawn from human relationships. They are essential for preserving the mystery of God and preventing childish misconceptions which, very understandably, people reject.

There is another point which is rather more disturbing. C. S. Lewis put it in his characteristically clear and vivid way:

> I sometimes wonder if we have even begun to understand what is involved in the very concept of creation. If God will create, He will make something to be, and yet to be not Himself. To be created is, in

some sense, to be ejected or separated. Can it be that the more perfect the creature is, the further this separation must at some point be pushed? It is saints, not common people, who experience the 'dark night'. It is men and angels, not beasts, who rebel. Inanimate matter sleeps in the bosom of the Father. The 'hiddenness' of God perhaps presses most painfully on those who are in another way nearest to Him, and therefore God Himself made man, will of all men be by God most forsaken?[1]

This makes it clear that there may be times when although we feel totally devoid of the divine presence, abandoned by God except at that point we don't think there is a God to abandon us, in reality, through seeking to be faithful to the way of faith and love and hope, we are in fact closer to God than at any time before. Being emotional creatures, we tend to seek a 'nice feeling' of God present with us, a feeling of quiet or a feeling of ecstasy. But feelings are beside the point: what matters is faithfulness to Christ. Christ on the cross apparently felt totally abandoned. Yet in the light of the resurrection his life is revealed to be eternally at one with his heavenly Father, and no more so than when he entered into the darkness consequent upon human sin on the cross.

It is not always possible fully to understand Simone Weil. But one always encounters in her writings a truth that both disturbs and draws us more deeply into the truth than we have been before. She wrote:

> 'He will laugh at the trials of the innocent.' Silence of God. The noises here below imitate this silence. They mean nothing.
>
> It is when from the innermost depths of our being we need a sound which does mean something – when we cry out for an answer and it is not given us – it is then that we touch the silence of God.
>
> As a rule our imagination puts words into the sounds in the same way as we idly play at making out shapes in wreaths of smoke; but when we are too exhausted, when we no longer have the courage to play, then we must have real words. We cry out for them. The cry tears our very entrails. All we get is silence.
>
> After having gone through that, some begin to talk to themselves like madmen. Whatever they may do afterwards, we must have nothing but pity for them. The others, and they are not numerous, give their whole heart to silence.[2]

The sceptical mind comes back at this point and asks what difference there is between this silence, the silence of God into which we enter by giving ourselves to silence, and the silence that exists because there is no God. There is no purely intellectual answer to this question, though the prior intellectual shaping of the mind will obviously influence how the silence is interpreted. Nor is the answer given through a difference in quality of the two silences. A person may cry out in disbelief and anger and it will still be the silence of God.

A remarkable novel by Anne Michaels, *Fugitive Pieces*, is pervaded by a terrible sense of loss: lost cities, lost people, terrible deaths and ordinary deaths. But it is not without hope. 'We look for the spirit precisely in the place of greatest degradation.'[3] When the gas ovens of Auschwitz were opened, people were found pressed against the wall still trying to climb to the air, still hoping, still crying out.

> At that moment of utmost degradation, in that twisted reef, is the most obscene testament of grace. Or can anyone tell with absolute certainty the difference between the sound of those who are in despair and the sound of those who want desperately to believe? The moment when our faith in man is forced to change, anatomically – mercilessly – into faith.

Yet, if there is indeed a God, it would be odd if he had not given the believer something to sustain her through this deepening darkness. The believer would have remained a believer because there have been moments of illumination, moments when the light glimmered.

In our time the poet who has pursued most insistently and profoundly the theme of the apparent absence of God is the Welsh priest R. S. Thomas. He has written:

> It is this great absence
> that is like a presence, that compels
> me to address without hope
> of a reply.

Then again

> Why no! I never thought other than
> That God is that great absence
> In our lives, the empty silence
> Within.

Yet this absence, this silence plays a crucial role in the apprehension of the true God as opposed to the reinforcement of our projections. The poetry of R. S. Thomas follows a classical *Via Negativa*, cleansing the mind of false images and the heart of false desires. We are to wait upon God because 'The meaning is in the waiting.' Again, 'An absence is how we become surer of what we want' but even in R. S. Thomas there are moments of illumination, made that much more credible and authentic because of his resolute refusal to contrive feelings about God:

> Suddenly after long silence
> he has become voluble.
> He addresses me from a myriad
> directions with the fluency
> of water, the articulateness
> of green leaves.[4]

The columnist Katharine Whitehorn once quoted some words of her father. 'Faith is life lived on the evidence of its highest moments.' Those highest moments provide the evidence in the light of which we seek to live a life of faith and love.

In 'The Four Quartets' T. S. Eliot quotes St John of the Cross almost verbatim in describing the *Via Negativa* through which we approach God:

> I said to my soul, be still, and wait without hope
> For hope would be hope for the wrong thing;
> Wait without love
> For love would be love of the wrong thing;
> There is yet faith
> But the faith and the love and the hope are all in the waiting.
> Wait without thought, for you are not ready for thought:
> So the darkness shall be the light, and the stillness the dancing.
> Whisper of running streams, and winter lightning.[5]

As those last lines suggest, not all is darkness. There can be points of light and moments of illumination. But in another section of the poem he takes up the same theme:

> For most of us, there is only the unattended
> Moment, the moment in and out of time,
> The distraction fit, lost in a shaft of sunlight,
> The wild thyme unseen, or the winter lightning
> Or the waterfall, or music heard so deeply
> That it is not heard at all, but you are the music
> While the music lasts. These are only hints and guesses,
> Hints followed by guesses; and the rest
> Is prayer, observance, discipline, thought and action.[6]

The moment when we are taken out of ourselves by the beauty of nature, the insights of a work of art, the nobility of a friend or the peace of mind that comes through prayer, are 'only hints and guesses'. The rest is a way of life pursued faithfully to the end.

CHAPTER 21

The Biggest Question of All: Suffering and a God of Love[1]

> If the sufferings of children go to make up the sum of sufferings which is necessary for the purchase of truth, then I say beforehand that the entire truth is not worth such a price . . . we cannot afford to pay so much for admission . . . it is not God that I do not accept Alyosha. I merely most respectfully return him the ticket.
>
> (Dostoevsky)[2]

> Strange blessings never in Paradise
> Fall from these beclouded skies.
>
> (Edwin Muir)[3]

There are many people who would love to believe that behind this strange universe of ours is a God of love – but they simply can't. The extent of human suffering in all its forms, emotional and spiritual as well as physical, is just too much. We can go further than this and suggest that an initial impulse to believe that there is a wise and loving power behind life is entirely natural. Children brought up in a stable, happy home see their parents as good, and it is natural for them to think that behind the life which they experience as good is a good creator. But however natural such a movement of the heart and mind might be it continually gets dashed and smashed to bits by some new tragedy, personal or seen on the television. This difficulty is perhaps particularly acute for those who see themselves as spiritual. For they are aware of a spiritual dimension to life, they touch within themselves a power to care for others, they don't believe that life can be ultimately meaningless but they find it very difficult to associate the capacity to love, which they know within themselves, with a universe that contains such cruelty and horror.

It is always dangerous to make comparisons between one period of history and another, nevertheless I suspect that we are more aware of the problem of suffering today than our forebears were. Life for them was hard, harder than it is for most people in the developed world today. But pain tended to be accepted as part of the scheme of things. Society as a whole offered a religious explanation of this and it was assumed by everyone that this life anyway was simply a preparation for another one beyond this. Today, by contrast, we don't accept that pain is an inevitable part of the scheme of things. We have powerful anaesthetics and painkillers which can control much of the pain that our forebears had to put up with. In that sense we are more sensitive to pain. Furthermore, we are daily bombarded by pictures on the television and in our newspapers of our fellow suffering human beings, children starving or dying of AIDS, villages being bombed and the bereaved mourning their dead. The explanations which were at least available for our forebears, that suffering was a punishment for our sins or a way of testing or improving our character, not only seem unbelievable, they come across as gross and certainly not congruous with any recognizable concept of love. It is true that in some ways we can better understand the inevitability of pain and suffering in any form of existence. This means that the question posed by suffering takes a new form, posed particularly sharply in Ivan in Dostoevsky's novel *The Brothers Karamazov* quoted at the head of this chapter. What it amounts to is questioning whether God was justified in creating the world at all. If he knew that creation would involve so much torment, was he justified in taking the risk, even if there is bliss at the end of it?

Since the holocaust the whole attempt to justify the ways of God to humanity, which is what theodicy has traditionally been about, has been regarded as deeply suspect. Theodor Adorno (1903–69), the German sociologist, said that there can be no poetry after Auschwitz. If there can be no poetry there can certainly be no theology in a traditional sense. Auschwitz forces us to face evil in all its horror and the only possible response is pity, anger and resolve never to let anything like that happen again. Art and theology, from this perspective, are at best distractions and at worse false consolations which blunt the reality we should be facing. Yet Adorno also said, 'There is nothing innocuous left . . . there is no longer beauty or consolation except in the gaze falling on horror, withstanding it, and in unalleviated consciousness of negativity holding fast to the possibility of what is better.' In that attitude; in facing horror squarely yet holding fast to the possibility of what is better, there remains still a place both for art and for faith: not beauty as escapism, not theology as false consolation trying to pretend things are not as bad as they seem, but beauty in that unblinking gaze itself and in the holding fast; consolation in the fact that, despite everything, there is within us the capacity to hold fast to the possibility of what is better. Theology, at its most authentic, undergirds and strengthens both the unblinking gaze and the capacity to hold fast to the possibility of something better.

The religious mind is naturally inclined to put a good gloss on things. A young woman died in particularly tragic circumstances and her mother said to me that she supposed God wanted her daughter more in heaven than she did on earth. I had to say, gently, no. The death of her daughter was a tragedy, plainly contrary to the will of God. The events of 11 September and all that has followed from them have for many people brought about a new awareness of the reality of evil in the world and a sharpness to their awareness of human suffering. Yet the human mind still looks for consolation. Since 11 September in New York a poem by the Polish writer Adam Zagajewski has been much quoted. Part of it goes:

> Try to praise the mutilated world
> Remember June's long days,
> And wild strawberries, drops of wine, the dew.
> The nettles that methodically overgrow
> The abandoned homesteads of exiles.
> You must praise the mutilated world . . .
> You have seen the refugees heading nowhere,
> You have heard the executioners sing joyfully.
> You should praise the mutilated world.[4]

It is good that when we are feeling depressed about the world, as we might very well be by the apparently endless cycle of violence in the Middle East, we should indeed remember June's long days: despite everything there are still moments of happiness. Yet that poem worries me insofar as it suggests that the memory of good moments can simply be juxtaposed with inhumanity and atrocities. For refugees need to be housed and executioners need to be stopped and it is not obvious that the memory of June's long days impels us to make an appropriate response. What is needed is not a softening of the consciousness of cruelty by letting it be bathed in the light of June's long days, but a fiercer sense of moral protest, of anger, of outrage and a resolve to change things for the better. If we leave aside Karl Marx's dialectical materialism, what gave his political philosophy such widespread appeal was its underlying moral protest against false consolations, both in the form of a misplaced hope and theologies which seek to justify the world as it is rather than change it for the better.

Christianity has always had a powerful awareness of the reality of evil. It has, we might say, rubbed our nose in doctrines of the fall and original sin. All is blighted, all is warped. Yet Christianity has always offered hope – not just hope for heaven but hope that humanity can co-operate with God in his unceasing work of trying to bring good out of evil. Authentic theology helps us both to face the evil and call it evil and strengthens our resolve to change the world for the better by undergirding that resolve with hope and divine help.

'Don't kill me, mum.' These were the last words of an eight-year-old boy as his mother pushed him under the water in the bath and drowned him. Some years before this she had killed her two young babies but it was thought, mistakenly, that she was now in her right mind and her older boy was safe. Such incidents which, alas, we can read about every day, rock any religious faith we might have to the foundation. How on earth can there be a God of love behind a universe in which such appalling things happen?

The case against the idea that there is a power of love behind the universe is very strong. Indeed someone has suggested that the situation is like a detective story. All the evidence appears to point to a particular culprit but the good detective, by using his intelligence, is able to see that the situation is very different. So it is in life. On the surface all the evidence seems to point against the possibility that love created the universe. Droughts, famines, car crashes, murders, cancer, mental illness, senility – all these add up to a formidable case to answer. Yet, by careful thought this case can be answered and in the course of answering it surprisingly strong evidence *for* the idea of a God of love emerges.

The price of free will

First, an obvious point. Much suffering in the world is caused by the negligence, weakness and deliberate wrongdoing of human beings. If it is the will of God to create free beings, as opposed to robots or puppets, this is the price he and we have to pay. It is true that some philosophers have suggested that God could have created us free in such a way as we always freely choose to do right. On this view God would be like a hypnotist who told us all under hypnosis how we should act. We would think we were deciding things for ourselves but in fact we would have been programmed by God. It would have been quite possible to create a universe in which this happened. But there is one fatal flaw. God himself would know he had cheated. He, at least, would know that we were not acting with genuine freedom but only in response to suggestions given us under hypnosis.

If we value being able to make up our own minds and make our own decisions in life then we too have to pay the price of living in a world in which this is possible. We cannot have it both ways. We cannot both be free and have a world in which wrong choices do no damage. This point, if accepted, has wide implications. For much more suffering in the world is attributable to human beings than we sometimes allow. Take the millions of starving. The fact is that there *is* quite enough food in the world for everyone. But through millions of wrong choices which have brought about the rigid political and economic structures in which we live, there are mountains of surplus food in Europe and America, while those in Africa starve to death. Similarly, take the question of earthquakes. The rich can afford to live in earthquake-free areas or in reinforced houses. It is the poor who cannot move or protect themselves. It is the poor who suffer.

Disease and earthquakes

So a great deal of suffering in the world is caused by human beings. But not all of it. There is disease. There are natural disasters. Two points can be made about this. First, God does not simply make the world: he does something much more sophisticated. He makes the world make itself. He gives everything in the universe, from the sub-atomic particles of which matter is composed, through electrons, atoms, cells up to multi-cellular structures like ourselves, a life of its own. In fact, when we think about it, a life of our own is the only kind of life we could have. If we did not have a life of our own we would not exist at all, and this is as true of the atom and the amoeba as it is of us. God has given the basic elements of matter a life of their own and has weaved the universe from the bottom upwards through the free interplay of millions of forces. In all this interplay, what we call accidents occur the whole time. But accidents are not in themselves harmful. Take the question of volcanoes and earthquakes. These occur because the planet called earth, on which we live, has reached a particular stage in its cooling. This is also the stage which made it possible for life to emerge. If the earth were still molten there would be no life. It has in fact cooled enough to allow a crust to form, on which life has been able to develop. But because it is a crust and not a solid ball the inner plates of the earth are still free to slide about a little, and the molten material inside the earth can on occasion find a way out of the crust. There is nothing wrong with these movements and eruptions in themselves: they are just examples of the millions and millions of clashes and combinations that occur every second at every level of the universe. They are not essentially different from the billowing of clouds or the movements of water in a stream.

God and the laws of nature

The second point is that in order to exist as the kind of creatures we are, capable of thinking and choosing, we need a relatively stable environment. I plan my day and make decisions in it on the basis of certain well-founded assumptions: that the sun will come up, that the laws of gravity will operate, that water will boil at a certain temperature and freeze at another one. The consequences of what I do – putting on the electric kettle or putting water in the freezer – are predictable. This means that there is a very strict limit on what God can do in the way of disrupting these scientific laws without frustrating his whole purpose in making the universe in the first place. It might be amusing to live in an Alice in Wonderland type of world but our amusement would only last a few seconds. If we suddenly started to shrink in an uncontrollable way or float up to the ceiling we literally would not know whether we were coming or going. If we were born into that kind of environment we would never learn to think at all, for thinking necessitates continuity between one day's experience and the next. If a child went to school and was told that the sign 'A' symbolized an 'aa' sound and the next day was told that the same sign really indicated a 'zz' sound, that child would never learn to read, for learning involves building on present experience in a predictable way. So it is with our environment as a whole. Sometimes we long for God to 'intervene' to stop some terrible accident in a miraculous way, but where would it stop? Suppose you are driving along and a young child runs out in front of the car. Normally you would hit the child – but a miracle occurs and you pull up short in ten feet instead of the expected 30 feet. That would be wonderful. But what about the car just behind you? In order to prevent that car bumping into you, another miracle would have to occur. And what about the car behind that one? In other words, a single alteration of the laws of nature (which are only laws in the sense that they are observed regularities on the basis of which we can make predictions) would have ramifications throughout the universe. And would it be fair to limit the miracle to one tiny point? If a miracle was performed to enable the first car to pull up in a few feet but not the second one, the driver of the second one could very well claim that it was unjust, for he had been driving along at the correct speed allowing for a proper stopping distance at that speed. He had not taken into account that a miracle would occur just in front of him – and why should he?

The self-limiting of God

This is not in any way to deny that God works in his universe. According to Christian belief he is at the very heart of things, closer to us than our own breathing. Furthermore, he works out his purpose through us, particularly when we co-operate with him in prayer. Indeed prayer itself may allow God to work through us in his universe in mysterious ways that we are not fully aware of. Nor is it to deny that full-blooded miracles, in the sense of a suspension of the laws of nature, may sometimes occur. The point is that there is a very severe limit to what God can do in this way without spoiling what it is all about – namely bringing into existence creatures like you and me, who are capable of thinking for ourselves and making real choices. For in order to exist as the kind of people we are, we need an environment characterized by continuity, stability, regularity and predictability.

The question arises, however: why did God make us as part of a material world? Much suffering arises from the fact that we are vulnerable creatures of flesh and blood, set in an environment whose regularity often seems very hard, as when a river floods and drowns many people. Why did not God simply create us as free spiritual beings like angels? No one really knows the answer to that question except God. All we can do is guess. The best guess comes from Austin Farrer. He argued that God bound us up with a physical universe in order to preserve our freedom in relation to himself. If we had been created like angels and set in the immediate presence of God we would have no freedom to respond to him or not. We would be drawn by his incandescent beauty and holiness like moths to a candle or metal filings to a magnet. So, in order that we might have real freedom of manoeuvre, God put us at a distance from himself – not a physical distance, because that is impossible, as God is closer to us than we are to ourselves – but a distance of knowing. He made us physical beings in a physical world to act as a kind of veil between us and himself. The result is that on this earth we have no immediate and overwhelming knowledge of God. Furthermore, we are born with a strong drive to preserve our life in being. We only come to a knowledge of God at all insofar as we are capable of growing out of our self-centredness and are willing to live before one who, by definition, makes a total difference to our lives. The knowledge of God is rarely overwhelming and inescapable. For most people there is only a flickering, dawning awareness which is always related to our willingness to know and love God. In this way God preserves our freedom and ensures that the pilgrimage we make is our own journey. (This guess has two implications, both of which I accept. First, angels are not as free as human beings. They are totally transparent to the bidding of God. Second, there was no fall of angels, for they were created perfect in the immediate presence of God.) We, however, have not been created perfect. We have instead been created with the possibility of achieving perfection of a different (and higher) kind than the angels. And we have not been created in the immediate presence of God. We have been made in such a way that we have to make our journey towards him.

So God has created a physical universe, which makes itself from the bottom upwards in ever more complex forms of life, until *we* emerge, as part of that physical universe, yet with the possibility of developing as rational, moral and spiritual beings; half ape, half angel, as Disraeli put it. The physical universe is characterized by reliability and predictability. We are now, for example, beginning to be able to predict hurricanes, earthquakes and volcanoes, and to take steps to avert their worst effects on us.

The actions of God

But what, we might say, is God doing in all this? First, God is holding the whole universe in being and enabling each tiny constituent part of it to go on being itself. We tend to take this for granted. But why should each electron, atom and cell of the universe both be there and go on retaining its essential characteristics in such away that it can combine to form higher forms of life? Religious believers claim this is so only because God, the source and fount of all being, holds everything in existence and does so in a way that reflects his own constancy. For the laws of nature, which we think of as so hard and impersonal, almost as an iron necessity, in fact reflect God's undeviating constancy and faithfulness. When the steam arises from a boiling kettle, or raindrops fall from the sky or a breeze dries the washing, these are expressions of the faithfulness of God, his steady constancy, his utter reliability.

Second, God himself feels the anguish of the universe. It is of the very nature of love to enter imaginatively into the situation of others and, to some extent, feel what they feel. God who is perfect love knows every point of the universe from the inside and bears it within his heart. The word 'sympathy' comes from two Greek words meaning 'to suffer with'. God suffers with his creation. When Jesus was tortured to death this was an expression, in human terms, of the pain God bears eternally.

Third, God is ceaselessly at work bringing good out of evil. When a tragedy occurs he inspires first sympathy and then practical action. He never stops in his work of making accident and disaster yield some good.

Fourth, the purpose of God cannot finally be defeated. Christ died a terrible death on the cross, apparently feeling that God had abandoned him. 'My God, my God, why hast thou forsaken me?' But God raised him from the dead to live for ever in a new kind of way altogether, as an ever-present spiritual presence. The purpose of love cannot finally be defeated.

Fifth, God has promised us an eternal existence with himself. He knows each one of us through and through and he will recreate our real self in a form appropriate to an eternal existence. Heaven lies ahead for those who will appreciate it.

A God of love

The case against the idea that there is a God of love behind the universe *is* very strong; indeed so strong that it *is* only on the basis of these five points, taken together, that it is possible to hold such a belief. Belief in eternity can hardly be an optional extra, for example, when so many people die young with their potential unrealized. If there is no further state beyond this life for them to develop in, how can we believe there is a God of love?

Similarly, if Christ was not raised from the dead how can we believe either in him or the God in whom he trusted? For he trusted his heavenly father to the bitter end, even through the darkness of despair. It is only on the basis of these five points that we can believe that love made the world.

But these five points are also the evidence for the love of God. They provide not only the case for the defence but evidence for positive belief. The evidence that there is a God of love is based on our belief that the world has a genuine independence. We are not a dream of God or simply an expression of his body. His love is so great that he has made a world with a life of its own and brought to the light of consciousness creatures who even have the power to frustrate his purpose. But this is not an indifferent, impassive God. God bears our travail and anguish within himself: so much so that he has come among us and experienced as a human person the worst that life can do. Yet this is not a God who was irresponsible enough to make a world over which he would lose all control. Making the world was a huge risk, but it was a risk he took in the confidence he could bring it to its natural fulfilment. Of this the resurrection of Christ is the expression and pledge. God's love cannot be defeated. He raised Christ from the dead and he will recreate each one of us anew for an eternal existence. As a father gives his children good gifts, so God will share with us his own immortality made manifest in Christ. This is very powerful evidence *for* the love of God. Believing in a God of love does not mean that horrible things do not happen. They do happen, all the time, for the reasons outlined earlier. The evidence for a God of love comes from a different source, from the five points just stated.

Is it worth it?

Although it is possible to understand some of the reasons why, if God was going to make creatures like us, the world has to have more or less the character of the world we know, it is still possible to wonder whether it is all worth it. 'Don't kill me, mum.' Was God really justified in creating a world in which he knew such things would happen? For even if there is an eternity ahead of that murdered child, nothing can change the fact that he was killed by his own mother and that he knew what was happening to him. This is the question of Ivan, one of the brothers in Dostoevsky's novel, *The Brothers Karamazov*. After recounting various stories of cruelty to children he asked if God was justified in making such a world. He then went on to argue that whatever harmony might be achieved in some heavenly future, nothing could justify such cruelty to children on the way. It wasn't that he disbelieved in God, he said. He just wanted to return his ticket. This is a powerful point, yet at least three things can be said which put a somewhat different perspective on the matter.

First, the question of whether life is worth it or not is a question each one of us has to answer for himself. No one can reply for us and we cannot presume to answer for them, however ghastly their circumstances seem to us. For when we come across someone in hospital, perhaps paralyzed from the neck downwards, our instinctive reaction is that we could not bear to live life under such conditions: we would rather be dead. Yet often such people show extraordinary courage and even cheerfulness, enhancing life for others in a most moving way. Whether, despite everything, life is worth living is a question only they can answer.

Second, the courage and endurance which so many show in life seem to witness to the fact that something desperately important is at stake in human existence, that it is not simply a matter of weighing up the pleasure against the pain. If it was simply a matter of weighing up the pleasure against the pain, far more people would commit suicide. But the vast majority of people do not commit suicide: they go struggling on with humour and fortitude, their lives, as someone once said, like flowers growing in a bed of concrete. In D. H. Lawrence's novel, *Sons and Lovers,* Paul Morel visits his mother, who is dying of cancer, and she chides him because his life is all struggle. She says she wants him to be happy. But Paul says that there is something more important than happiness and unhappiness: he wants to live. By that he did not mean live it up. He wanted to live with all the courage and creativity within him.

Third, there are sometimes experiences in human life when a glorious goal makes the difficult journey to it seem worthwhile, as when a runner after years of hard training wins a gold medal at the Olympic Games. Or there are times when a glorious experience can make the pain of the past drop away, as when an engaged couple who have been separated for a year and only able to communicate by phone and letter come together again. All the pain of missing one another and the inevitable misunderstandings fade into the background.

If at the end of the whole creative process, beyond space and time, when, as St Paul puts it, God is all in all, everyone who has ever lived is able to bless God for their existence, then the unbiased critic must admit that God was justified in taking the risk of creating a universe. For all who have gone through the experience will say for themselves, 'Praise the Lord O my soul, all that is within me, praise his holy name.' This would be heaven. Of course suffering will not be totally forgotten. In the stories of Christ's appearance to his disciples, the wounds remain. But they are healed and transfigured, taken into a new, deeper reality in which they too have a part to play. This vision of an ultimate state of affairs in which all is well is a hope. But it is a hope that is witnessed to not only by the Christian faith but by the practical example of countless millions of people, of all faiths and none, who live lives with great courage. For they seem to have an intuitive sense that something vastly important is at stake in all this human travail. In old-fashioned language, what is at stake is the making of our eternal souls.

A practical answer

On Karl Marx's grave in Highgate Cemetery are carved his famous words 'Philosophers have only interpreted the world, the point is, however, to change it.' Christians have much sympathy with that statement; for they do not offer a philosophical answer to the problem of suffering, as though it were something to be resigned to – they offer a vision of an ultimate state of affairs in which suffering as we know it no longer exists, a state of affairs which has to be worked for. It is true that the new heaven and earth of which the Bible speaks go beyond our space and time, but they have to be reached for and built up on this earth. The answer to the problem of suffering is not an idea or a theology but an actual state of affairs, which does not yet exist, but which offers us a vision of what, under God, can come about if we co-operate with God in his work. There are some very important practical implications of this.

First, suffering is contrary to the will of God. In the gospels Jesus is shown healing the physically and mentally sick, casting out demons, calling sinners to change their ways. His ministry is an invasion of the forces of goodness and light against all that blights and hurts human life. There may be a sense in which God is responsible for everything, in that he created the universe. But a sharp distinction has to be made between what God directly wills and what he merely permits as part of his overall purpose. So a parent may be responsible for giving his child permission to drive the family car. But he in no sense wills the subsequent accident that unfortunately occurs. God wills the universe to exist, he lets it be with a life of its own. But he does not will suffering; on the contrary, he opposes it. Christ, the image of God, brings life and health. So Christians, following his example, have founded hospitals, leper colonies, hospices and all manner of institutions dedicated to relieving the sick.

Second, God is ceaselessly at work bringing good out of evil and we are called to co-operate with him in this task. For it is the particular work of God not only to oppose all that mars human life but to make what mars our lives yield some good fruit. So sickness can bring about sympathy and practical support from friends and a deeper understanding of life from the sufferer. Here we have to be very careful. While it is true that many good qualities and actions can come out of sickness or tragedy, God does not design horrible situations in order to bring this good out of them. Such a God would be intolerable. If a friend tripped us up on the stairs and broke our leg in order to see whether we would develop qualities of patience and endurance under adversity we would not think much of her friendship: indeed we would not call her a friend. So with God. God, like a good friend, wants things to go well with us. He is not about to pull the carpet from under us to see how we will react. For good breeds more good than evil can. A comfortable home, with enough to eat, caring parents and an interest in sport or culture is much more likely to give children a chance to develop as healthy personalities than a home that is impoverished or stricken in one way or another. The parents in such a home may be very caring but if they are continually worried about money, have little time to give to their children because they have to work so hard, if they live in poor physical surroundings or are stricken with mental illness, then the children are likely to be affected. Good breeds more good than evil can. It is the particular mercy of God to make even evil yield some good.

Everyone knows someone who under adversity has developed admirable qualities. We have all been involved in tragic or difficult situations which have brought the best out of people. This is all summed up in some lines of the poet Edwin Muir. He contrasts our sad world with the apparently perfect conditions of the garden of Eden, but concludes:

> But famished field and blackened tree
> Bear flowers in Eden never known.
> Blossoms of grief and charity
> Bloom in these darkened fields alone.
> What had Eden ever to say
> Of hope and faith and pity and love . . .
> Strange blessings never in Paradise
> Fall from these beclouded skies.

There is a tightrope to walk here. God does not will suffering. On the contrary, he wills us to relieve and eliminate it, so far as we can. Yet out of suffering can come hope and faith and pity and love. God did not design the beclouded skies in order that strange blessings might fall from them. Yet fall they do, making life look very different. The weighing of goods and evils is notoriously difficult and should not be done. A husband who has just lost a dearly loved wife does not want to be told that he has become a much deeper, more understanding person as a result: he would rather have his wife back. A man whose son has been killed in a motorbike accident may spend the rest of his life helping youth clubs and do much good work: but he would rather have his son back. Yet, if there is an eternal destiny, the good which people see coming out of evil will one day find its proper place. For if we have been made to grow more and more like God, so that we can live with him in the Communion of Saints, the deepening of a person in a bereavement or the good work that people undertake as a result of tragedy are considerations of ultimate significance.

Living in faith

The thoughts put forward here are only of very limited use and no use at all when a person is in anguish. When a person is afflicted with physical or mental pain they want understanding and practical help: they do not want religious consolation or attempts to 'justify the ways of God to men'. Nevertheless, there is a limited use for the kind of considerations adduced here on other occasions. For, as has been admitted, the case against the idea that love made the world is a formidable one. Unless something sensible is said, faith can ebb away and hope die. There is no intellectual solution to the problem of suffering and certainly no knock-down arguments. All that is possible is to say enough to go on living in faith and hope and love. For, paradoxically, the very strength of the case against the notion of a God of love reveals more clearly the evidence for a God of love. This evidence, as considered earlier, has five features. First, God has given us a real independence. He has created us rather than dreamt us. Second, God himself feels our anguish with us. Third, he is ceaselessly at work forcing even evil to yield some good. Fourth, as the resurrection of Christ reveals, his purpose cannot finally be defeated. And fifth, God has promised us an eternal existence, if we are ready to receive it. A character in a novel by Rebecca West says at one point, 'What's the good of music if there's all this cancer in the world?' To this someone else responds, 'What's the harm of cancer, if there's all this music in the world?' Music can lift people into a dimension in which life seems very different. This is even more true of the love of God. A knowledge of the love of God does not stop tragedy being tragedy or suffering suffering. There is no glossing over, no pretending that all is for the best. For manifestly all is not for the best; a great deal is for the worst. But the love of God, of which we all have some practical proof in the sheer existence of our own being, but which is definitively disclosed in the life, death and resurrection of Christ together with the promises to us inherent in Christ, is a kind of music which makes us see, in our best moments, what really matters and what does not matter quite so much.

There is no intellectual solution. Instead, the Christian faith offers a vision of what the love of God is in the course of achieving. We are called to co-operate with that love by relieving suffering, eliminating its causes in poverty and disease and by responding to things going wrong in as constructive and positive a way as possible. For so it is that God's purpose is furthered. A sense of how much suffering there is in life can lead us to deny our maker or to care for his world. The more we care, the more conscious we will be of the affliction which besets us. But the more we care the more certain we will be that the world which is afflicted is good. And in caring we will be at one with the caring of God.

As Austin Farrer has written:

> An overmastering sense of human ills can be taken as the world's invitation to deny her maker, or it can be taken as God's invitation to succour his world. Which is it to be? Those who take the practical alternative become more closely and more widely acquainted with misery than the onlookers; but they feel the grain of existence, and the movement of the purposes of God. They do not argue, they love; and what is loved is always known as good. The more we love the more we feel the evils besetting or corrupting the object of our love. But the more we feel the force of the besetting harms, the more certain we are of the value residing in what they attack; and in resisting them are identified with the action of God, whose mercy is over all flesh.[5]

Christianity teaches that in Christ, God comes close to us, makes himself accessible to us in order to win us over to himself and draw us into the heart of light. To respond, in particular to respond to the clear call of Jesus to follow him in giving God's just and gentle rule absolute priority in our lives, is to experience a sharpening of the contrast between the world as it is and the world as it could be. It is to share a hallowed grief. But Jesus said 'Blessed are those who mourn.' For to enter into the pain of the world and to do what we can to alleviate it – through prayer, through use of our resources, through action which is both personal and political – is to heighten both a sense of the value of the world and of the ground and giver of its value, and to be taken into the beauteous love that lies behind it.

Epilogue

This World is not Conclusion,
A Species stands beyond –
Invisible, as Music –
But positive as Sound –
It beckons, and it baffles –
Philosophy – don't know –
And through a Riddle, at the last –
Sagacity, must go –
To guess it, puzzles scholars –
To gain it, Men have borne
Contempt of Generations
And Crucifixion, shown –
Faith slips – and laughs, and rallies –
Blushes, if any see –
Plucks at a twig of Evidence –
And asks a Vane, the way –
Much Gesture from the Pulpit –
Strong Hallelujahs roll –
Narcotics cannot still the Tooth
That nibbles at the soul –

(Emily Dickinson)[1]

With this in mind, then, I kneel in prayer to the Father, from whom every family in heaven and on earth takes its name, that out of the treasures of his glory he may grant you strength and power through his Spirit in your inner being, that through faith Christ may dwell in your hearts in love. With deep roots and firm foundations may you be strong to grasp, with all God's people, what is the breadth and length and height and depth of the love of Christ, and to know it, though it is beyond knowledge. So may you attain to fullness of being, the fullness of God himself.

(Ephesians 3.14–19)

Notes

Introduction

1 R. S. Thomas, 'The Empty Church', in *Collected Poems 1945–1990* (J. M. Dent, 1993), p. 349.
2 David Hay and Kate Hunt, *Understanding the Spirituality of People Who Don't Go to Church* (Centre for the Study of Human Relations, University of Nottingham, August 2000).
3 Alec Vidler, *The Church in an Age of Revolution* (Penguin, 1961), p. 113.

1 The Despot God

1 Private letter to the author from Louis de Bernières.
2 Brian Keenan, *An Evil Cradling* (Vintage, 1992), p. 187.
3 Simone Weil, *Gravity and Grace* (Routledge, 1963), p. 79.
4 Austin Farrer, *Said or Sung* (Faith Press, 1960), pp. 34–5 included in *The One Genius*, selected by Richard Harries (SPCK, 1987), p. 30.
5 W. H. Vanstone, *Love's Endeavour, Love's Expense* (Darton, Longman and Todd, 1977).
6 Boswell's *Life of Johnson* (Everyman, 1963), Vol II, p. 146.

2 The Male Boss

1 Alice Walker, *The Color Purple* (Women's Press, 1983).
2 Daphne Hampson.
3 D. H. Lawrence, *'Stand Up!'*, *The Complete Poems*, ed. Vivian De Sola Pinto and Warrant Roberts (Heinemann, 1964), Vol. I, p. 560.
4 Shakespeare, *Troilus and Cressida*, I, iii, 110–124.
5 I have written more fully on the relationship between hierarchy and equality in Richard Harries, *Is There a Gospel for the Rich?* (Mowbray, 1992), pp. 106–12.
6 *The Rule of St Benedict*, trans. by Justin McCann (Sheed and Ward, 1976), p. 70.
7 Eucharistic Prayer G, in *Common Worship* (Church House Publishing, 2000).
8 Janet Morley, 'Eucharistic Prayer for Ordinary Use', in *All Desires Known* (Movement for the Ordination of Women and Women's Theology, 1988), p. 40.
9 Henri Nouwen, *The Return of the Prodigal Son* (Darton, Longman and Todd, 1992).
10 C. F. Andrews: letter to Rabindranath Tagore on the occasion of the poet's birthday, May 1915, quoted by Nadir Dinshaw in *A Wide-Open Heart* (Christian Action, 1992), p. 51.
11 Dinshaw, *A Wide-Open Heart*, p. 64.
12 Dinshaw, *A Wide-Open Heart*, p. 64.

3 Eternal Punishment

1 Stevie Smith, *'How Do You See?'*, *Collected Poems* (Allen Lane, 1975), p. 517.
2 Boswell's *Life of Johnson* (Everyman, 1963), Vol. II, p. 526.

3   Richard Harries, 'On the Edge of Universalism', in *Julian, Woman of our Day*, ed. Robert Llewelyn (Darton, Longman and Todd, 1987), pp. 41 ff.
4   William Golding, *Pincher Martin* (Penguin, 1956), p. 184.

4 The Oddness of Praise
1   Dean Inge.
2   Auberon Waugh, *The Sunday Telegraph*, 18 April 1999, p. 39.
3   Austin Farrer, 'The End of Man, in *The One Genius*, selected by Richard Harries (SPCK, 1987), p. 153.
4   Quoted by John Moorman, *Richest of Poor Men* (Darton, Longman and Todd, 1977), p. 24.
5   A. N. Wilson, *God's Funeral* (John Murray, 1999), p. 304.
6   Peter Shaffer, *Equus* (Andre Deutsch, 1973), pp. 78–9.
7   T. S. Eliot, 'The Dry Salvages' from 'The Four Quartets' in *The Complete Poems* (Faber, 1969).
8   Susan Sontag, *The Guardian Weekend*, 27 May 2000.

5 Why Did It All Begin?
1   Evelyn Waugh, *Decline and Fall* (Penguin, 1980), p. 33.
2   Shakespeare, *King Lear*, IV, i, 36.
3   C. S. Lewis, *A Grief Observed* (Faber, 1961), p. 26.
4   *The Poems of Gerard Manley Hopkins*, ed. W. H. Gardner and N. H. McKenzie (OUP, 1970), p. 90.

6 Does God Have Favourites?
1   Shakespeare, *Hamlet*, V, ii, 10.
2   John Henry Newman, *Meditations and Devotions* (Longmans, 1907).

7 What About Good People Who Are Not Christians?
1   Quoted by Tim Hilton in *John Ruskin: The Early Years* (Yale University Press, 1985 and 2000), p. 254. See also his 'Burlesque of Protestantism', in Tim Hilton, *John Ruskin: The Later Years* (Yale University Press, 2000), p. 495.
2   Hilton, *John Ruskin: The Early Years*, p. 74.
3   Richard Harries, *Art and the Beauty of God* (Mowbray, 1993 and 2000).
4   Jonathan Sacks, *Faith in the Future* (Darton, Longman and Todd, 1995), pp. 241 and 242.
5   Aung San Suu Kyi, *Freedom From Fear* (Penguin, 1995), p. 233.
6   Aung San Suu Kyi, *Freedom From Fear*.
7   Krishna Dutta and Andrew Robinson, *Rabindranath Tagore* (Bloomsbury, 1995), p. 227.
8   Rabindranath Tagore, *Gitanjali* from *Collected Poems and Plays* (Macmillan, 1958), p. 4. See also pp. 18 and 44 for the two earlier quotations from Tagore.
9   Nelson Mandela, *Long Walk to Freedom* (Little, Brown and Co., 1994), Part 1.
10   'Jews, Christians and Muslims: The Way of Dialogue', in *The Truth Shall Make You Free* (the report of the 1988 Lambeth Conference), Appendix 6.
11   Rowan Williams, *On Christian Theology* (Blackwell, 2000), p. 173.
12   Austin Farrer, quoted in Richard Harries, *The One Genius: Reading Through the Year with Austin Farrer* (SPCK, 1987), p. 50.
13   Williams, *On Christian Theology*, p. 38.

8 Why the Cruelty and Horror In Nature?
1   Richard Dawkins, *Unweaving the Rainbow* (Penguin, 1998), p. 18.
2   In particular I would commend the books of John Polkinghorne, Arthur Peacock, Russell Stannard and Paul Davies.
3   Richard Dawkins, *The Blind Watchmaker* (Longman, 1986), pp. 11 and 13.
4   Steve Jones.
5   Eucharistic Prayer G, in *Common Worship* (Church House Publishing, 2000).
6   Samuel Taylor Coleridge, *The Rime of the Ancient Mariner*.

7 Austin Farrer, *A Celebration of Faith*, ed. Leslie Houlden (Hodder and Stoughton, 1970), p. 61.

9 Religion Is Stuck In the Past
1 *Selected Prose of T. S. Eliot*, ed. Frank Kermode (Faber, 1975), p. 38.
2 T. S. Eliot, 'Little Gidding' from 'The Four Quartets', in *The Complete Poems and Plays* (Faber, 1969), p. 197.

10 Religion Is Divisive
1 Algernon Charles Swinburne, *On the Russian Persecution of the Jews*.
2 David Martin, *Does Christianity Cause War?* (OUP, 1997).
3 Hans Küng, *Global Responsibility: In Search of a New World Ethic* (SCM, 2003), p. xv.

11 Religion Keeps People Immature
1 Dietrich Bonhoeffer, *Letters and Papers from Prison* (Fontana, 1962), p. 108.

12 Life Today Is Just Too Good for Religion
1 David Starkey, *The Sunday Telegraph Review*, 21 September 1997, p. 4.
2 Nick Hornby, *How to be Good* (Viking, 2001), p. 184.
3 Letter to Sir George Beaumont, 28 May 1925.

13 Christianity Is Anti-Life
1 Algernon Charles Swinburne, 'Hymn to Prosperine'.
2 James Joyce, *Portrait of an Artist as a Young Man* (Penguin, 1956).
3 Wilfred Owen, 'Maundy Thursday', *War Poems and Others*, ed. Dominic Hibberd (Chatto and Windus, 1963), p. 55.
4 R. S. Thomas, 'The Minister', *Song at the Year's Turning* (Rupert Hart-Davis, 1955), p. 92.
5 T. S. Eliot, 'The Love Song of J. Alfred Prufrock', in *The Complete Poems and Plays* (Faber, 1969), p. 14.
6 Shakespeare, *As You Like It*, II, vii, 139.

14 Christianity Bangs On About Guilt and Sin
1 Ludovic Kennedy, *All in the Mind: A Farewell to God* (Hodder and Stoughton, 1999), p. 5.
2 Rose Macaulay, *The Towers of Trebizond* (Collins, 1956), p. 16.
3 Thomas Hardy, 'Surview', *The Complete Poems* (Macmillan, 1976), p. 698.
4 T. S. Eliot, 'Little Gidding' from 'The Four Quartets', in *The Complete Poems and Plays* (Faber, 1969), p. 194.
5 T. S. Eliot, 'Little Gidding'.

15 Christians Eat God
1 Ludovic Kennedy, *All in the Mind: A Farewell to God* (Hodder and Stoughton, 1999), pp. 37–8.
2 George Herbert, 'Love', in *The Complete English Works*, ed. Anne Pasternak Slater (Everyman, 1995), p. 184.

16 Christianity Is Just for Wimps
1 C. H. Sisson, 'A Letter to John Donne', in *Collected Poems* (1984), p. 66.
2 R. S. Thomas, 'The Priest', in *Collected Poems* (Dent, 1993), p. 196.
3 *A Grief Observed*, p. 10.

17 Our True Self
1 Steve Bruce, *Choice and Religion* (Oxford University Press, 1999), p. 162.
2 See article on *Theosis* in *The Oxford Dictionary of Byzantium* (Oxford University Press, 1991), Vol. 3, p. 2069; Timothy Ware, *The Orthodox Church* (Penguin, 1963), pp. 236 ff.
3 Rowan Williams, *On Christian Theology* (Blackwell, 2000), p. 287.

18 Re-creating Humanity
1   Austin Farrer, sermon preached in 1991 and printed in *Theology* (May/June, 1991).
2   'Apologue on the Parable of the Wedding Garment', in Charles Williams, *The Image of the City* (Oxford University Press, 1958), p. 167.

19 On Not Saying Too Much
1   C. G. Jung, *Memories, Dreams, Reflections* (Collins, 1967), p. 63.
2   John of Damascus, 'Exposition of the Orthodox Faith' I, 4, *Nicene and Post-Nicene Fathers* (Eerdmans, 1983), Vol. IV.
3   Pseudo-Dionysius, *Complete Works*, trans. Colm Luibheid (Paulist Press, 1987), pp. 49–50.
4   Hilary of Poitiers, 'On the Trinity', II, 2, *Nicene and Post-Nicene Fathers* (Eerdmans, 1983), vol. IX.
5   Eric Griffiths, 'What's Wrong with Roger Scruton?', *The Times Literary Supplement*, 9 July 1999, p. 3.
6   Emily Dickinson, *The Complete Poems*, ed. Thomas H. Johnson (Faber and Faber, 1970), p. 506.
7   W. H. Auden, 'The Truest Poetry is the Most Feigning', in *Collected Poems* (Faber and Faber, 1976), p. 470.
8   Dietrich Bonhoeffer, *Letters and Papers from Prison* (SCM, 1962), p. 160.

20 The Silence of God
1   C. S. Lewis, *Letters to Malcolm Chiefly on Prayer* (Fontana, 1964), p. 46.
2   Simone Weil, *Gravity and Grace* (Routledge, 1952), p. 102.
3   Anne Michael, *Fugitive Pieces* (Bloomsbury, 1998), pp. 167, 168.
4   R. S. Thomas, 'The Absence', in *Frequencies* (Macmillan, 1978), p. 48; 'Via Negativa', in *H'm* (Macmillan, 1972), p. 16; 'Kneeling', in *Not That He Brought Flowers* (Rupert Hart-Davis, 1978), p. 32; 'Abercuawg', in *Frequencies*, p. 26; 'Suddenly', in *Later Poems* (Macmillan, 1983), p. 201. These poems can also be found in his *Collected Poems*.
5   T. S. Eliot, 'East Coker' from 'The Four Quartets', in *The Complete Poems and Plays* (Faber, 1969), p. 180.
6   T. S. Eliot, 'The Dry Salvages' from 'The Four Quartets', p. 190.

21 The Biggest Question of All: Suffering and a God of Love
1   The substance of this chapter was first written in the form of a booklet for the Christian Evidence Society. It was reproduced in Richard Harries, *Questioning Belief* (SPCK, 1995).
2   F. M. Dostoevsky, *The Brothers Karamazov* (Penguin, 1976), Vol. 1, p. 287.
3   Edwin Muir, 'One Foot in Eden', in *Collected Poems* (Faber and Faber, 1960).
4   Adam Zagajewski, 'To Praise the Mutilated World', tr. Claire Cabanagh, originally published in the *New Yorker*, 24 September 2001.
5   Austin Farrer, *Love Almighty and Ills Unlimited* (Collins, 1966), p. 188.

Epilogue
1   Emily Dickinson, 'This World is not Conclusion', *Complete Poems* (Faber, 1975), p. 243.